Cuba's Island of Dreams

University Press of Florida

Gainesville Tallahassee Tampa Boca Raton Pensacola Orlando Miami Jacksonville

Cuba's Island of Dreams

Voices from the Isle of Pines and Youth

Jane McManus

05 04 03 02 01 00 6 5 4 3 2 1

LIBRARY OF CONGRESS CATALOGING-IN-PUBLICATION DATA
McManus, Jane.
Cuba's island of dreams: voices from
the Isle of Pines and Youth / Jane McManus.
p. cm.
Includes bibliographical references and index.
ISBN 0-8130-1741-6 (cloth: alk. paper)
1. Isla de la Juventud (Cuba)—History. I. Title.
F1799.I8 M36 2000
972.91'25—dc21   99-043006

The University Press of Florida is the scholarly publishing agency
for the State University System of Florida, comprising Florida
A&M University, Florida Atlantic University, Florida
International University, Florida State University, University of
Central Florida, University of Florida, University of North Florida,
University of South Florida, and University of West Florida.

University Press of Florida
15 Northwest 15th Street
Gainesville, Florida 32611–2079
http://www.upf.com

For Bill
and our best friend, Rufus

Contents

Preface   ix

Prologue   1

1. The American Occupation   17

2. The Long Depression   50

3. Changing the Face of the Isle   97

Epilogue: Daughter of the Caribbean   168

Notes   171

Bibliography   175

Index   183

Preface

The Isle of Youth (formerly Isle of Pines) off the south coast of the main island is the second largest in the Cuban archipelago, with a unique history that has been largely ignored. Here to help rectify that situation are the voices of ordinary people describing their not-so-ordinary experiences as residents there throughout the twentieth century. Their individual perspectives, recorded during the crisis years of the 1990s, highlight the changes that have taken place since 1959 and what occurred in earlier years. To underpin and supplement this oral testimony, I searched out the Isle's recorded history in Cuba's archives, libraries, institutes, and research centers and in books, magazine articles, and pamphlets published in English in the United States. Generous Cuban historians and researchers shared their unpublished papers. Librarians in both countries were solicitous in locating hard-to-find materials.

As I read, I soon got caught up in the dreams of the pirates, ranchers, soldiers, prisoners, and foreign visitors who made its male history over four centuries. That history is summarized here in a prologue that provides the backdrop for one woman: Evangelina Cossio Cisneros, leader of the only rebellion on the Isle of Pines during the Cuban independence struggle. Her dream of freedom—for her country, for herself—is the appropriate introduction to *Cuba's Island of Dreams*. In the prologue's historical summary, I have avoided using endnotes. However, in the section on Evangelina Cossio Cisneros, I have specified sources (almost all out of print) that contribute to historical, political, and feminist interpretations of an incident that resonated as late as 1925. Of particular relevance to this section is the interview, recorded in 1990, with a second-generation native of the Isle of Pines whose father was one of the resident insurgents of 1896.

In the immediate aftermath of that war, the American invasion of Cuba brought occupation troops, jurisdictional hamstringing, private investments, and immigration. On the Isle of Pines, the American presence was particularly notable. It is documented in chapter 1 from a wide range of written sources—Irene Wright's objective survey titled *Isle of Pines* (1910); the tattered issues of the weekly *Isle of Pines Appeal*, edited by the fulminating annexationist E. de Laureal Slevin from 1911 to 1925; the Supreme Court's decision in *Pearcy v. Stranahan*; the history of the Hay-Quesada Treaty; Hart Crane's poem about the 1926 hurricane—as well as by the oral histories relating individual dreams.

In chapter 2, the Model Prison is the fulcrum and symbol of the long depression that lasted from the Machado military dictatorship of the 1930s to the fall of Batista in 1959. More nightmare than dream, the Model Prison was the subject of investigation and criticism by historians, civic leaders, and political prisoners all through that period. Among the latter were Fidel Castro and his rebel comrades who attacked the Moncada Garrison in 1953. An earlier inmate, Mosako Harada, describes his incarceration there during World War II for the crime of being Japanese. British-born Peggy Rice recalls a very different war-related experience on the Isle during that same period.

Chapter 3, covering the postrevolutionary period, constructs the changing face of the Isle from oral history played against development strategies, demographic charts, research papers, newspaper reports, and my own on-site observations. Although some interviews took place as early as 1986 and the last in 1999, the main in-depth conversations were recorded in April–May 1990, when I spent nearly a month on the Isle with my husband, Bill Brent; our long-haired dachshund, Rufus; and our Lada to get us around.

We lived in an apartment in downtown Nueva Gerona, right across from the hospital (which we visited out of curiosity rather than need) and two blocks from the Institute of Friendship with the Peoples (ICAP), whose attentive Magaly Reyes Espinosa arranged our housing and ration card, facilitated trips and appointments, and dispensed information. Historian Juan Colina la Rosa stopped by almost daily to answer questions and suggest additional sources of information. On previous visits to the Isle, he had introduced me to most of the old-time residents I talked to again and again during that month, and he continued his help on every subsequent visit. Juan and Magaly form an integral part of my research efforts. I talked to both of them every time I went to the Isle.

From 1991 on, my trips there were briefer and more sporadic—three or four days once or twice a year—but I always followed up on the friends I made in 1990. Their oral histories are inserted according to the topic and period under discussion, rather than date of interview, since the interview methodology was in-depth and open-ended rather than question and answer. Thus their perceptions and experiences may corroborate, contradict, or offer a different perspective on the written word.

The voices of the Isle recorded over a dozen years span a century of its history, the richest and most complex. The older voices that speak from as far back as the first decade of the twentieth century have now been silenced by death, and their interviews with me are the last—often the only—testimony they recorded. Here I present them all, immigrants, natives, and foreign students:

Andrés Fernández Soto is the son of one of the *pineros* captured during the abortive uprising organized by seventeen-year-old Evangelina Cossio during Cuba's War of Independence. After he returned from prison, the elder Fernández designed and built the family's Spanish-style home in Nueva Gerona. Father and son built the Sundstrom bungalow across the way. Interviews with Andrés took place in 1990 and 1999.

Andrés Fernández Soto at the carved door of the house his father built in 1912

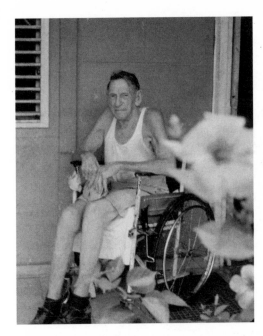

Harry Koenig (1904–1995), the last American on the Isle

Harry Koenig, the last American immigrant on the Isle, died there in 1995. He was five years old in 1909, when his German American parents moved down from Cleveland, Ohio, with their three children. Harry's brother Willy was born on the Isle in 1910; then came Gertrude and, finally, Paul. Of the six siblings, Harry and Willy remained on the Isle. My first interview with Harry was in 1990 at his bungalow in Nueva Gerona.

Vasily Rachek was born in the Ukraine, "when that part of it was Polish." After World War I, the family moved first to the United States, then to the Isle of Pines, where brother Ramón was born. The brothers live on an isolated farm not far from Sylvia Baker's house and became part of her support group after she was widowed. I interviewed Vasily at Sylvia's house in 1991.

Edith Sundstrom was fourteen in 1920, when her Swedish American parents came from Massachusetts to join relatives on the Isle of Pines. She married another Swedish American and lived happily on

Edith Sundstrom's bungalow as she left it in 1987

the Isle until her husband and parents died. She returned to the States in 1987, and I interviewed her in Miami in 1991.

Bertha Maud Tatum Jackson was six in 1905, when her family sailed from the Cayman Islands to the south coast of the Isle of Pines. She married Moddriel Jackson, whose father, Atkin, founded Jacksonville and persuaded other Cayman Islanders to buy into his modest real estate venture. Maud's neighbor Dick Hydes was a baby when his Cayman parents, like the Tatums, exchanged one poor island for another. Interviews with both of them were recorded in Cocodrilo in 1990.

Mosako Harada, elder statesman of the Japanese colony, died in 1999, at the age of ninety-five. He arrived in Santa Clara in 1925 on a year's contract and managed to get to the Isle in 1926 to start farming and learning Spanish. His Japanese wife, Kesano, came in 1929 by previous arrangement with her father, and died on the Isle in 1994. The Haradas always spoke Japanese at home, and their children responded in kind, but the grandchildren and great-grandchildren understand only Spanish. I first interviewed them in 1990, on their farm in Júcaro.

Maud Jackson, born in Cayman, at home in Cocodrilo, 1990

Dick Hydes, a Caymanian neighbor

Mosako and Kesano Harada on their farm in Júcaro, 1990

Jamaican Sylvia Baker was twenty-four when she left home for Cayman and the Isle of Pines. It was 1929 and she needed a job and a good man. She found both within the Isle's extensive English-speaking community, so she never bothered learning Spanish. After her husband's death, Sylvia lived alone but near good neighbors on the outskirts of Santa Barbara. I interviewed her several times between 1990 and 1993. She died on the Isle in 1994.

Rulle and Annie Ebanks, *pineros* of Cayman descent, lived among English-speaking Cayman and Jamaican immigrants from the time they were born. Forced to learn Spanish because of their ten children, who were all born after 1960, they continued speaking English with older relatives and neighbors like Sylvia. Rulle died of a stroke in 1992. I interviewed them in 1990.

Mongo Rives was born on the Isle and began playing music with his *pinero* father when he was a youngster. Now in his sixties, Mongo Rives and his Tumbita Criolla are a part of the Isle's cultural patrimony with their traditional *sucu-suco*. The group rehearses in the patio of Mongo's home in Santa Fé, where I visited him in 1999.

Jamaican Sylvia Baker (left) with Rulle and Annie Ebanks, Cubans of Cayman parentage

La Tumbita Criolla, with Mongo Rives, director, wearing straw hat

Above: Peggy Rice at ninety, with Lobo and (l. to r.) son-in-law Armando Valdés, great-granddaughter Jackie, granddaughter Margarita Valdés, and friend Julio

Left: Peggy Rice in the American Cemetery

Peggy Rice sailed down from Nova Scotia with her husband and their two young boys in 1931. She died in 1992 at the age of ninety-one, the last British resident on the Isle. Peggy's granddaughter Margarita (Shug) Valdés Rice is a second-generation *pinera* who speaks English with her Gran's clipped accent. Shug's mother, Joan Rice (1939–1976), her father, Armando Valdés, and her daughter, Yaqueline (named for Jacqueline Kennedy) Mayal Valdés, were all born on the Isle, as was Jackie's father, José Antonio Mayal. Interviews with the extended Rice family were recorded from 1990 to 1999, mostly at their home in Patria.

Virginia Baca Baca is a direct descendant of the black militiamen and their families resettled on the Isle of Pines from the Spanish garrison in St. Augustine in 1832. I interviewed Virginia in 1996 at the telephone post in Los Colonos.

Lydia McPherson, island-born daughter of Jamaican parents, is the mother of six daughters, who live and work on the Isle. I interviewed Lydia in 1991, when I was staying at Las Codornices Motel, where she worked. She retired shortly after that and died in 1998.

Eduardo Hanzawa is the engineer grandson of one of the thirteen important families that make up the Japanese Association on the Isle and an associate in the family cooperative. I interviewed him in 1996.

Foreign students Manuel Fernández Fala from Angola, Alfred Ackom from Ghana, and José Dina from Mozambique talked about the difficulties and rewards of student life on the Isle. Oscar Ellejalde Villalón, director of the Teachers' Training College, provided an overview of the foreign students' program. The interview with the director took place in 1992. The students were interviewed in 1995.

Daniel García came to the Isle in 1970 to do his social work as an art teacher, and stayed. Among his colleagues and former students are Amelia Carballo and Angel Norniella Santos, who founded the ceramics group Terracota 4 on the Isle, then moved their workshop from Nueva Gerona to Old Havana. I first interviewed Daniel on the Isle in

1990 and caught up with him several times over the years up to 1999. Amelia and Angel were interviewed in Old Havana in 1997.

I am grateful to all these people for sharing their dreams and experiences. Tapes and transcripts of their interviews are deposited in the Word Fund of the Pablo de la Torriente Brau cultural center of Havana, directed by Victor Casaus, in appreciation of the *Memoria* award for oral research I received in 1997. My husband, Bill Brent, who accompanied me on several trips and interviews, has been unstinting in his support and encouragement throughout this project. Frances Goldin, friend and literary agent, was generous—as always—with her suggestions and solutions. Special thanks go to Sheryl Lutjens and Tom Miller, whose separate and sometimes convergent comments were invaluable in making final revisions.

Prologue

On June 13, 1494, during his second voyage to the Americas, Admiral Christopher Columbus, in the vanguard of three caravels, sighted land he claimed in the name of the Spanish Crown and christened El Evangelista, considering it part of the Asian continent he had found on his first voyage. Columbus and his men remained on the isle for thirteen days of hunting and observation. To the Spaniards everything was new and unfathomable, though they tried to relate what they saw to what they knew. Thus, crocodile and turtle footprints in the sand were those of fantastic lions; and a flock of feeding cranes, seen at a distance between pines and pot-bellied palms, was a group of monks in religious robes. Later navigators charted the shores of what soon came to be known as the Isle of Pines, and naturalists cataloged its treasures.

An aeon before Columbus's thirteen-day exploration of that terrain, long before the Guanahatabey Indians beached their canoes and painted enigmatic symbols in sheltering caves on the isle they knew as Camarco, it was joined to Cuba's southwest coast. At some point in time it cut loose and became separated from the bigger island by a shallow sixty-mile-wide gulf. Geographic isolation and social abandonment were the handmaidens of its underdevelopment.

The early European immigrants who displaced the shy nomadic Indians were eliminated by marauding pirates in plundering attacks that continued over more than three centuries. British corsair and slave trader John Hawkins landed on the Isle of Pines in June 1565 and forcefully provisioned his ships; Francis Drake came ashore in 1596 and wiped out the incipient Spanish settlement there; Henry Morgan made countless Caribbean forays to the Isle of Pines before he died in Jamaica in 1688. Their compatriot William Dampier rediscovered the Isle at the end of the seventeenth century and described its notable geographic features for England's rulers. Sporadically, Dutch, French, and Portuguese corsairs also concealed their booty along its coasts and bartered or bullied for food and fresh water.

In 1576, the Crown had ceded ownership of the island to an influential subject named Jerónimo Rojas y Avellaneda, who gave it to his brother Hernán Manrique de Rojas because of the latter's interests in fleeting a squadron to protect island waters. Neither of the brothers paid any attention to the Isle, though Hernán's son Francisco built the first chapel there. The Isle was still virtually unpopulated in 1762, when the British seized Havana and occupied it for nearly a year before returning it to Spain in exchange for the Florida peninsula.

Two centuries after the first Rojas became its owner, the Isle of Pines still belonged to one family descendant, named Nicolás Duarte, who divided the northern part into seven circular haciendas and willed each one to a son, along with his eleven slaves. In 1792, the

Isle had only eighty-six inhabitants, according to the study Dionisio Franco made after his British captors dropped him off there.

The scattered ranchers and fishermen were virtually defenseless—until 1822, when a fearless pirate-in-residence named José Rivas, better known as Pepe el Mallorquín (Joe from Majorca) took on the enemy. With the approval of the Spanish Crown and Isle of Pines residents—including his mistress, Rosa Vinageras—Pepe and forty men aboard his armed schooner sank the flagship of the British fleet at the delta of the Júcaro River, near the settlement of Santa Fé. The British returned the following year, mired the schooner in coastal mangroves, and mortally wounded the resident pirate. Pepe el Mallorquín managed to reach his woodland refuge, where he died in the arms of his mistress. His death marked the end of piracy, which no longer suited the British lords of the sea. Within a few years, that legacy of plunder and skulduggery became an adventure classic in the fictional *Treasure Island,* penned by Scots writer Robert Louis Stevenson (1850–1894).

The settlement of Santa Fé existed as early as 1809, while Nueva Gerona (named in honor of Captain-General Francisco Dionisio Vives, who had defended the Catalan city of Gerona) was founded in 1830 as the capital of the new colony of Reina Amalia (Queen Amalia was the third wife of the reigning monarch, Ferdinand VII). By that date, there were no public lands available for colonization, and the Crown was forced to seek land donations for the colony from the *hacendados.* "To promote the white population," the government offered settlers tax exemption for fifteen years and promised to build a garrison, a church, and a cemetery. Yet, five years later, the colony had only 378 inhabitants.

A French chemist and geologist named M. Chueaux reached the Isle in 1834, attracted by reports of gold. When he discovered the marble cliff of Mount Caballos, he abandoned his search for gold and obtained permission from the Spanish to establish a quarry at the edge of the

Brazo Fuerte stream, where he also built his residence and planted his gardens. While digging in the garden one day, Chueaux discovered what he thought was a vein of gold-bearing quartz. He went to Havana to record his claim and died there of yellow fever.

Chueaux's quarry, machinery, residence, and gardens stood idle until 1844, when Captain-General Leopoldo O'Donnel, governor of Cuba, bought the property. O'Donnel erected a great mill equipped with American machinery and built extensive docks in Colombo Bay. Prisoners from the Gerona penal colony were paid ten cents a day to work the marble. The first block they cut was carved into a baptismal font and presented to Nuestra Señora de los Dolores (Our Lady of Sorrows) parish church in Nueva Gerona. When O'Donnel's opponents in Spain pushed through a tax on sea sand, used in cutting the marble, the company collapsed.

In 1860, the Island Development Society was formed to promote new enterprises and services, the medicinal springs and other health facilities, a regular steamboat route, and increased tile production. The society brought in forty-eight Chinese on eight-year contracts to produce tiles for construction. During the Civil War in the United States (1861–1865), when Cuba was unable to import from the north, the Isle of Pines shipped tiles and agricultural products to Havana. With the resumption of trade between the United States and Cuba, the Isle lost its Havana market because of high shipping costs. Small businesses failed, and most of the Chinese workers left.

The advent of the 1868 independence war on the main island was the coup de grâce as far as development went. Already, the Isle was infamous as a dumping ground for Havana's undesirables: urban vagabonds and delinquents, chained to construct the garrison and other public buildings in Nueva Gerona that made it the administrative and military center.

Santa Fé, in contrast, was recommended as a health spa as early as 1857, in a memoir by Cuban doctor José Luz Hernández published after several years of medical research and experimental farming at his Cayo Bonito estate near Santa Fé. Dr. Luz was struck by the absence of cholera, malaria, and yellow fever on the Isle, which he believed was due to the pure air. Not one of the 400 Spanish soldiers sent there for temporary acclimatization in 1855 had succumbed to any of those diseases, said Luz, while troops on the main island were decimated by them. For patients suffering from tuberculosis, tumors, liver problems, and dermatological disorders, he recommended a diet of bland meat—that of the endemic *majá* boa he considered ideal—avoidance of all internal and external stimulants, and daily drinking and bathing at the Santa Fé springs near his home.

Felipe Poey, Cuba's most eminent botanist at that time, was another enthusiastic booster. While cataloging flora and fauna on the Isle, he described the springs as "crystal clear with a high composition of solvent iron, good for any afflictions."

The most convincing American propagandist for "the miraculous waters of its mineral baths" was Samuel Hazard. He boarded at Santa Fé's modest Santa Rita hotel in 1866 and chronicled his visit in *Cuba with Pen and Pencil*. Hazard claimed he was completely cured of bronchial affectations in ten days, without giving up smoking. Perhaps because of the climate, other patients found the springs more beneficial than those of Carlsbad and Saratoga Springs.

During the Ten Years' War (1868–78), the Spanish Lieutenant-General Valeriano Weyler took leave of his military duties on the main island to soak his aches and pains at El Respiro, a Santa Fé spring bubbling with calcium, magnesium, sodium, potassium, and other curative elements. The fount was thereafter known as Weyler's Spring.

Major José María Sardá, a wealthy Catalan engineer, had meanwhile acquired Brazo Fuerte and the Colombo Bay docks. He discontinued work in the marble quarry, but established a brick yard, tile works, and a tannery at Brazo Fuerte, which operated with fifty slaves and some twenty deportees. Sardá's tiles, made of sandy clay from terraces near Nueva Gerona, floored Morro Castle and were used in the public market building of Havana. Sardá also held, in concession, the Havana rock quarries where seventeen-year-old José Martí was sentenced to labor in shackles for his anticolonial views. At the request of Martí's father, an old friend, Sardá had the young prisoner transferred to the Isle of Pines in 1870 and welcomed him at El Abra, his plantation home.

According to census figures for 1868 and 1878, the resident population of the Isle of Pines hovered around 2,000, nearly two-thirds white. Of the 700 blacks, 480 were slaves (slavery wasn't abolished until 1886), 27 were emancipated slaves, and 194 were free blacks. In the latter category were the families of 78 militiamen from the Spanish fort of St. Augustine, Florida, pensioned by the Royal Crown and resettled on the Isle of Pines in 1835, in the newly founded colony of Reina Amalia. Their rocky terrain has ever since been known as Los Colonos.

Of the white population, a handful of ranching families still owned the Isle's original seven great haciendas and their sub-divisions— called *hijas* and *nietas* (children and grandchildren)— and a larger number of poor peasants worked the land as squatters or small farmers. Blacks as well as whites were overseers, artisans, tradesmen, and fishermen. For years after Britain and the United States officially outlawed the international slave trade in 1803, the Isle was used as a clandestine way station for African slaves. On the Isle, the captives were fattened up to bring a better price at slave auctions in New Orleans that continued up to the Civil War in the United States.

During both periods of Cuba's independence wars, scores of young fighters captured in battle and independence sympathizers were deported to the Isle of Pines. In May 1896 José Agustín Cossio y Serrano, a veteran of the Ten Years' War who had already spent a year in prison for aiding the insurgents of 1895, was deported to the Isle. He was accompanied by his two adolescent daughters, whose mother, Caridad Cisneros de la Torre, had died giving birth to the younger, Carmen. Of the 350 deportees in the penal colony at that time, 139 were self-supporting and lived outside the barracks, Cossio among them. Through his friends the Betancourts, who ran the local bakery, Don José was able to use one of the ovens to bake cassava bread to sell to the local population. Living quarters had also been prearranged in a multipurpose mud house just off the military square. The house was built around a common patio shared by a grocery store, a barbershop, a carpentry workshop, a doctor's office, a one-room apartment, and the Cossios' two-room space.

Discreetly, sympathizers began dropping by to welcome the veteran Cossio, meet his attractive young daughters, and talk about the war. Twenty-four-year-old Emilio Vargas, sent to the Isle after his capture in battle the previous June, and the baker's nephew Rosendo Betancourt told Evangelina about their involvement in the January escape of ten political deportees who had forced the captain of a fishing sloop to ferry them to the mainland coast. Vargas and Betancourt had pulled out at the last minute because they didn't think the escape would work. With hindsight, they blamed themselves for not having joined those "crazy kids," as General Antonio Maceo fondly called them after they appeared at his camp in Pinar del Río. Both young men eagerly committed themselves to the rebellion planned for July 26, during which Vargas and two other deportees were killed and Betancourt escaped.

FROM THE ISLE OF PINES TO THE WHITE HOUSE:
EVANGELINA COSSIO CISNEROS AND CUBAN INDEPENDENCE

Americans first learned of the case on August 14, 1897, when the *New York Journal* featured a front-page story and photo with a four-inch headline: "Cuba's Jeanne D'Arc. Pretty Evangelina Cisneros to Face 20 Years in African Dungeons. President Her Uncle. Girl's Father . . . Likely to Be Executed. Rebellion the Crime Alleged."

The *Journal* was owned by William Randolph Hearst, who purchased it in 1895 and began building circulation with his sensational promotion of Cuba's War of Independence, launched that year. Rebel Commander-in-Chief Máximo Gómez was said to prize the jeweled sword the *Journal* sent him and to value its coverage of his intrepid advances toward Havana as General Antonio Maceo stormed through Pinar del Río during the summer of 1896.

On July 26 of that year, seventeen-year-old Evangelina Cossio Cisneros led a daring uprising on the Isle of Pines, in which young exiled rebels and local hotheads risked their lives to join Maceo's troops. The date they chose was the feast of Santa Ana, when the soldiers would presumably be off guard, merrymaking in the streets. On the same feast day in 1953, rebels led by Fidel Castro attacked the Moncada Garrison in Santiago de Cuba. In neither case did Santa Ana support subversion.

To that wartime endeavor of national liberation, Evangelina added her own feminist claim to personal freedom from sexual harassment: she publicly rejected the commanding colonel's advances in a tryst trap set for him in her own house.

According to the military report of the rebellion issued by Spanish Captain-General Valeriano Weyler, "Some two hundred and fifty poorly armed men appeared in the streets of Nueva Gerona shouting subversive slogans, while a group of fourteen rebels kidnapped the Military Commander, Cavalry Lieutenant Colonel D. José Bérriz, and held him in a house, bound and under threat, until a patrol from the garrison attacked the place and released him to take command of his forces, thereby dispersing the mutineers after an hour and a half of fighting in which three rebels were killed. The uprising is completely under control and it is expected that the participants will soon be at the disposition of the authorities. The leaders are already in the hands of Lt. Col. Bérriz, according to the military commander of Batabanó, who went to reinforce the garrison with a naval infantry company and fifty civil guards."

The "poorly armed men" referred to in the military report—in greatly exaggerated numbers—were island-born residents of Santa

Fé who participated as a support group in the plan to capture Bérriz. Twenty-one of them were sent to La Cabaña fortress, along with Evangelina's father, when she was shipped to the Women's Prison in Havana.

Born in 1910, Andrés Fernández Soto is the son of one of those rebel *pineros*, the name for natives of the Isle of Pines. His father, father-in-law, uncles, and their cousins and friends were among the farm boys from Santa Fé who rode their horses into Nueva Gerona on that moonlit night in July 1896, brandishing machetes and shouting, "*Viva Maceo.*" In 1990, Andrés recalled in detail what he had heard from his father, Serafín Fernández García.

Andrés Fernández Soto

The rebellion was organized by pineros *and prisoners, with Evangelina as the leader. She was daring, a real* guapa *all right, ready to kill the commander; but the plot was to force him to surrender the garrison in Nueva Gerona so the rebels could get hold of the weapons there. After they were armed, they planned to take the next boat over to join Maceo's forces. They never intended to hold the fort. They just wanted to get to the battlefield.*

The reason the pineros *were all from Santa Fé was because it was the most important town, the port of the Júcuro River, where the ships came in; and famous people had been cured at its medicinal springs. Gerona was a penal colony and didn't develop until after the war. My father was born in Santa Fé in 1875, of Spanish immigrants. His father died when he was five years old, and a Spanish "friend" stole his mother's savings, so he started working as a kid. He did all kinds of work and worked for all kinds of people. Everybody knew everybody else in those days. The Isle was like one big family.*

Bruno Hernández was head of the group from Santa Fé and my father-to-be was second in command. They came across the bridge, turned on what is now Thirty-Second Street, and rode up to the corner of Thirty-Sixth and Twenty-Seventh Streets, past the Gómez house (a very well known house that has now been remodeled and looks great). At the corner, a Spanish patrol fired on them, and Bruno Hernández was killed right there. His crazy second, my pa, yelled, "Arriba!" (Carry on), but all they had to carry on with were machetes and knives.

Evangelina lived near there, at what is now the corner of Thirty-Ninth and Twentieth Streets. When the colonel entered her house, Emilio Vargas, the Pimienta brothers, and some other deportees grabbed him and tied him up. Then they heard the firing and ran out the back way. Berríz's men rushed in through the front door and freed him. Vargas and the Pimienta brothers were hunted down and killed. The authorities rounded up Evangelina and everybody else who had been involved or was said to have been involved in the uprising.

My father and twenty others in the Santa Fé contingent spent eighteen months in La Cabaña. It was very damp and some got sick. One of them died. They had no medicine so they melted candles and used the wax to relieve their chest pains. To pass the time, they all carved their initials on the cell walls. The only contact they had with home was by mail, but most pineros were illiterate in those days. My father had learned to read and write from the teacher in Santa Fé, so he wrote home to his girlfriend (my mother). That's when she learned enough to send an answer to her boyfriend in prison.

News of the thwarted uprising quickly spread among rebel fighters and prisoners. Evangelina was a heroine to them, as beloved and respected as their cause. The great Cuban troubadour Sindo Garay, a rebel army messenger in 1896, voiced their sentiments in his song "Evangelina, amor del patrio suelo" (Evangelina, love of the homeland).

If Evangelina was impressed by the commotion she had caused, she didn't show it during her imprisonment in the Women's House of Correction in Havana. Nor was she surprised to learn that the intermediaries sent by the president of the Republic in Arms, Salvador Cisneros Betancourt, an uncle on her late mother's side, and the diplomatic inquiries of U.S. Consul Fitzhugh Lee had failed to budge the Spanish military officials from their intention to try her in a closed military court. After Lee mentioned her case to the Havana correspondent of the *New York Journal*, though, things took a different turn.

When Evangelina completed her first year in prison in August 1897, the situation in Cuba was quite different from when she arrived. The Bronze Titan, General Maceo, had been killed in battle, and, though General Gómez controlled most of the island, his hungry, disheartened troops sometimes had to be whipped into battle. The ranks of Spanish soldiers, mostly young rookies with no heart for the fight, were decimated by disease and disillusion. General Weyler's reconcentration of the civilian population had resulted in such widespread starvation that he was generally referred to as the "Butcher." In the capital, wealthy Spanish loyalists remained adamant against autonomy, while wealthy Cubans pushed for the annexation that José Martí had preached must be avoided. The *mambises* on the battlefield were as committed as ever to Martí's goal of full independence from Spain and the United States, but the war had reached a stalemate.

These same positions and a few others were reflected in the United States, the country predestined to determine the outcome of the war without having reached a consensus on exactly how or precisely when. President William McKinley was for compromise with Spain to permit future investment, perhaps through autonomy. Naval adviser Theodore Roosevelt led a group that advocated America's "manifest destiny" over Spain's remaining colonies—Cuba, Puerto Rico, and the Philippines—through destruction of the Spanish fleet. The

Cuban delegation in New York was negotiating with a syndicate of bankers to buy independence, while shipping supplies to the independence fighters through a cordon of hostile Spanish and American vessels. The U.S. Congress mustered only minority support for recognizing the rebels or for intervening on their behalf. The U.S. public harbored a protective but unarticulated sympathy for the underdog Cuban liberation struggle, fed by the yellow press to build circulation and the political clout it represented.

Hearst, the master media mogul of them all, introduced into this volatile climate a dramatic and appealing symbol of *Cuba Libre*, so genuine and convincing that the usual exaggerations, distortions, and half truths he used as embellishment didn't really matter. Evangelina Cossio Cisneros was young, beautiful, well connected, brave, patriotic, and a prisoner of the "Butcher" Weyler. Nudged by Hearst, women all over the world took up her cause, with thousands of signatures on a clemency petition addressed to the Queen Mother of Spain. When that failed, Hearst upped the ante with the corpus delicti, dispatching his correspondents to rescue Evangelina from prison and smuggle her out of Havana aboard the steamship *Seneca*. She arrived in New York on October 9, 1897, and was whisked to a suite in the Waldorf Astoria hotel, where everybody who was anybody in New York called to welcome her.

Liberation of a foreign prisoner of war by a privately owned newspaper was unheard of, but this case was so eminent that it was gingerly discussed at President McKinley's next Cabinet meeting, resulting in "unofficial sentiments of sympathy" with the *Journal*'s release of Miss Cisneros. For further diplomatic protection, Evangelina signed an official Declaration of Intention to become a citizen of the United States, dated October 15 (duly reproduced in the *Journal*). That same day, her rescuer Karl Decker presented her in a thronged Madison Square, with fireworks exploding overhead. Later, she shook hands with a more select group of guests invited to a formal reception at Delmonico's. Illustrations of these events appeared in the

Journal, along with a picture of the grave heroine in the gown she wore for the occasion.

Barnstorming for Cuban independence, Evangelina helped raise funds for the Cuban delegation by selling bonds, stamps, and a silver peso souvenir coin bearing the legend *Patria y Libertad* above a profiled female head that many mistakenly assumed was Evangelina's. In fact, Leonor Molina, U.S. resident and cousin of the treasurer of the Cuban delegation, was the model for the portrait designed by an Italian sculptor.

In all these situations, Evangelina acted with dignity and poise. The only time she seemed at all fazed was when President McKinley received her in the White House. In his presence, Evangelina became tongue-tied and could only smile and shake his hand. The president was said to be greatly moved by her story.

As Evangelina appeared in public, the *Journal* kept her on its front pages with comments about her case from governors and mayors, statesmen and businessmen, members of the Cuban community and the women who had earlier signed the clemency petition. Readers devoured daily installments of the rescue from prison and the life story of the young woman who had become the nation's idol overnight as the symbol of *Cuba Libre.* (She was also the inspiration for the Cuban Amazon of Virginia Lyndall Dunbar's novel of that title, published in Cincinnati in 1897—in which the protagonist's battle for sexual equality and male gallantry drove her to a nunnery.)

The readers of the *Journal* were mostly poor and semiliterate; many were European immigrants with only a smattering of English. They bought the paper as much for the ads (bargain sales featuring solid oak dining-room chairs at $1.19 each; stag-handled carving sets with spring steel blades at $0.48; eight-day striking solid oak mantel clocks for $1.75; ladies' kid gloves in all colors and sizes, $0.79 per pair) as for the news. The *Journal* reached readers with all the elements of the story summarized in the headlines and presented in emotion-packed drawings by Frederic Remington and other top illustrators.

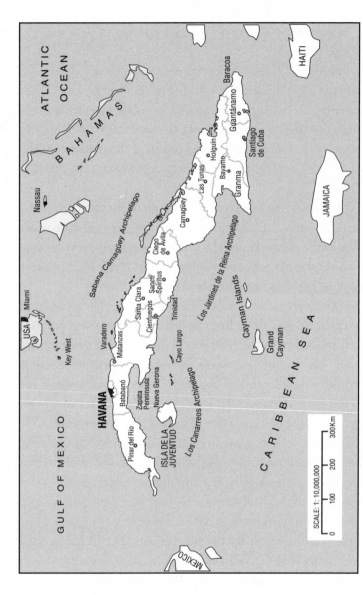

1. Cuba in the Caribbean

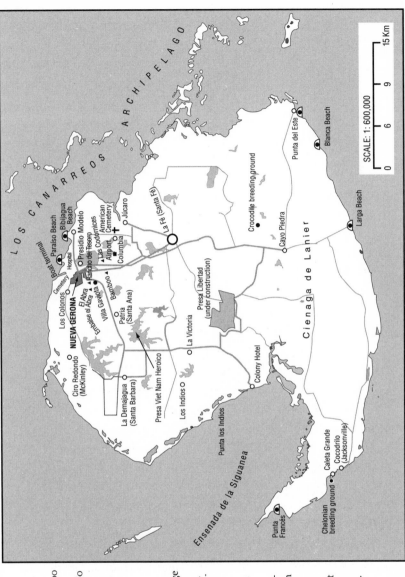

ISLE OF YOUTH

85,000: estimated population year 2,000

With an area of 1,180 sq. mi., it is the second largest island in the Cuban archipelago (total area 42,827 sq. mi.)

It has a mean average temperature of between 25 and 26.8°C. (77.4 to 80.2°F.) and two seasons: dry (November through April) and rainy (May through October, the month when most hurricanes occur). In general, the climate is sunny, hot and humid with refreshing sea breezes.

2. Isla de la Juventud

In large part, the *Journal* created the populist fervor to join in the Cuban independence struggle and fed it to the end, when "Remember the *Maine*" finally pushed the country to enter the fray. Hearst boasted that he spent a cool million on his *New York Journal* between 1895 and 1898 to bring on war. Whatever the cost, the promotion of Evangelina Cossio Cisneros was his finest hour.

Nor was it forgotten in later years. In 1925, Cuban ambassador to Washington Cosme de la Torriente y Peraza cited the rebellion in order to win Senate votes for ratification of the Hay-Quesada Treaty, recognizing Cuba's sovereignty over the Isle of Pines. Reconstructing the war period in *The Crime of Cuba* (1933), American historian Carleton Beals wrote, "One woman, Evangelina Cossio Cisneros, fired the American public with her miraculous escape from death." In *Cuba: the Pursuit of Freedom* (1971), British historian Hugh Thomas noted that "a new exploit of the *Journal* had taken precedence over the conflict, in the eyes of North Americans at least." Claude Julien, in *L'Empire Américain* (1968), even suggested that Evangelina was responsible for President McKinley's last-minute acceptance of the Teller Amendment to the U.S. Declaration of War on Spain, which legitimized Cuban sovereignty over the island once it was pacified.

After Evangelina's death in 1970 at age ninety-two, Cuban commentators tended to separate the rebel action from the Hearst promotion, praising the former and condemning the latter. Antonio Nuñez Jiménez, who buried Evangelina Cossio with military honors, also labeled her "a puppet in the hands of the merchants of the Hearst press" in his definitive book *Isla de Pinos: Piratas, Colonizadores, Rebeldes* (1976).

For Andrés Fernández, the uprising in its broadest scope is part of his heritage: "This young patriot's rebellion was recorded by the general of the Spanish army in Cuba, and also in the Senate of the United States. So it is truly part of our history. For my family, of course, it has special importance."

1 The American Occupation

Under the Treaty of Paris, ending the Spanish-American War of 1898, Spain surrendered its military and administrative control of Cuba to American occupation forces and ceded outright to the United States "Porto Rico and all other islands now under Spanish sovereignty in the West Indies." Exclusive U.S. hegemony over the Americas, claimed in the Monroe Doctrine of 1823, was finally established.

On January 1, 1899, a U.S. military government headed by General John R. Brooke occupied Cuba to pacify and sanitize[1] the island following a devastating war that liberated it from four centuries of Spanish colonial rule. Having completed their task, the occupation forces would withdraw and Cuba would become independent. The status of the Isle of Pines was not so clear-cut in February 1899, when General Brooke sent Major-General Fitzhugh Lee to inspect it. Was it under temporary occupation as a part of Cuba? Or was it one of those "other islands" ceded to the United States?

As U.S. consul in Havana in 1897, before America became a belligerent in Cuba's Independence War, Lee had been known as an annexationist with independence sympathies. He acted as the discreet intermediary for the escape of Spain's most famous prisoner of war, Evangelina Cossio Cisneros, while she was awaiting court martial for mutiny with intent to murder the Spanish military commander of the Isle of Pines.

After peace was ratified, Major-General Lee appointed as his aide an influential Cuban named Carlos Carbonell, who had smuggled Evangelina to the United States and married her there before they both returned to Cuba. Lee had more than enough background information for a knowledgeable inspection of the Isle of Pines.

In February 1899 Lee arrived aboard the cargo ship *El Protector,* thus establishing a regular maritime route that continued until the end of the U.S. occupation in 1902. It connected the Isle with Batabanó, on the south coast of Cuba, where United Railroads of Havana continued to the capital.

The Isle was a tranquil, almost deserted outpost then. A company of sixty insurgents under a captain had replaced the Spanish soldiers at the fort and were waiting to surrender it to U.S. Marines. All the rebel prisoners garrisoned there with Evangelina during the war and released in the general amnesty of 1898 were gone, but some of the native-born *pineros* who rebelled with her and served their time in Havana's La Cabaña fortress were back home on the Isle. They were among the 2,990 native Cubans counted in the 1901 census prepared by the U.S. War Department, which also listed 195 Spaniards and 14 other foreigners, including a few Americans.

Andrés Fernández Soto

My father and mother were married on January 1, 1900, in Santa Fé. Then my father had to find work to support the family

*they planned to raise. He did carpentry, masonry, laid water and
sewage lines, and eventually became an engineer in charge of
sanitation and other community works. He had to study to get
ahead; and he studied on his own because there weren't any secondary schools on the Isle, and it cost money to study in Havana. There was a lot of construction in Gerona then and he
liked that work. He built this house with all its columns, and we
moved here in 1912, when I was two. He built quite a few other
houses around here, too. When I was older, I worked with him.*

*In those days, the local businesses were owned by Spaniards,
Chinese, Americans—all foreigners. My father always told me:
"Get along with all of them and don't worry about the government. Devote yourself to your house, your family, your responsibilities, your work. Remember, honor knows no color."*

*I knew lots of the Americans here because, as I say, I got along
with everybody. Nationals of twenty-seven places lived here,
but the Americans weren't the biggest colony; the Japanese were.
People were called American even when they were English or
came from some other European country and spoke English.
There were Hungarians, Germans, Poles, Caymanians, Jamaicans, even a Peruvian family; and everyone got along. The Japanese were always very hard-working; the Chinese were very
commercial; and so were the gallegos.*

The term *gallego* refers to any Spaniard, not just a native of Galicia,
and they were the dominant foreign-born residents of the Isle at the
start of the twentieth century. Most of the Cuban-born residents
could also claim Spanish descent if they wished. Ten years later, Spanish heritage was recognized with the inauguration of a new Gallego
Club. The English-language weekly *Isle of Pines Appeal* reported that
the opening ball was showy: "300 electric lights of different colors, a
ten-piece orchestra from Havana, officials and prominent members of
the Club, which has 28,000 members in the West Indies, 170 of them
on the Isle of Pines."

Founded by an American settler named A. E. Willis in 1904 to further the cause of annexation, the *Isle of Pines Appeal* covered all local happenings and ran ads catering to the Americans who were building and furnishing their homes on acreage purchased in the United States from one of the land companies.

With a speculative eye on the unspecified "other islands" mentioned in the Treaty of Paris, a wealthy Tennessean named Samuel H. Pearcy set up the Isle of Pines Company in 1900.[2] Pearcy bought up more than 100,000 acres of land for between $1.75 and $2.00 an acre and began selling small tracts out of his New York office for up to $20 an acre. That was at least five times less than land values anywhere in the United States. He retained a sizable share of the south shore timber lands for exploitation. Aware of the advantages of direct shipping routes between the Isle and U.S. markets, Pearcy also established the Isle of Pines Transportation and Supply Company in 1904 and, in 1908, opened a monthly shipping route to Mobile, Alabama, via the company's Isle Line.

The Americans who bought land from Pearcy were convinced that the Isle of Pines had been ceded to the United States. They were simply moving to another part of their native land, not to a foreign country. The land companies, bolstered by the Platt Amendment, did nothing to disabuse them of that notion.

As a condition of withdrawing U.S. occupation forces, General Leonard Wood, Brooke's successor as military governor, insisted that the Platt Amendment be appended to the Cuban Constitution of 1901. Drafted by U.S. Secretary of War Elihu Root and introduced in the U.S. Congress by Senator Orville H. Platt of Connecticut, the amendment gave the United States virtual control over Cuba's foreign relations and the right to intervene militarily in the island's affairs from permanent naval bases.[3] It also omitted the Isle of Pines from Cuba's territorial boundaries, "the title thereto being left to future adjustment by treaty."

The United States relinquished the Isle of Pines to Cuba in a treaty drawn up the following year, but the treaty failed to be ratified by the U.S. Senate within the time specified. In 1904, John Hay for the United States and Gonzalo de Quesada for Cuba signed a second treaty identical to the first except that there was no time limit for its ratification. Strategically, the Isle of Pines was of no interest to the U.S. government, but it was virgin territory for American private entrepreneurs. Cuban land was devalued after the war, and there was no control on sales to foreigners.[4]

Other land companies followed Pearcy's example. Thomas Keenan, who purchased the Brazo Fuerte property from Sardá's widow and children at the end of the war, was a director of the Santa Fé Land Company, incorporated in Iowa with capital of $150,000.[5] Keenan's company, along with the Isle of Pines Land Development Company and the Almacigos Spring Company, bought up all the cattle-raising haciendas and resold them in subdivisions of 10 to 40 acres. The American Settlers' Association, the San José Company, and other entities also purchased large tracts for subdivision. By 1915 the seven original haciendas into which the Isle was divided in the mid-eighteenth century were transformed into some 10,000 American-owned farms that occupied 90 percent of the Isle's territory: approximately 363,000 acres of cultivable and wooded land.[6]

Yet American settlers were never a majority of the population. The 1907 census showed a total of 3,276 inhabitants, including 751 white foreigners, of whom 438 were Americans. The 1919 census showed 386 Americans among the 4,228 inhabitants. At that time Cuba had a total population of 2,889,004 and nearly 10,000 American residents.

Census figures for the period are much lower than population figures from other less official but more influential sources. The United Railways of Havana, in its promotional pamphlet *Cuba: A Winter Paradise* (1915–16 season), claimed the Isle of Pines had "4,851 registered American property owners and over 2,000 actual American residents and settlers," with a total population "a little short of 20,000." Perhaps heads were counted in both directions on the three overnight trips a week aboard the cruise ship *Cristobal Colón*, of the Isle of Pines Steamship Company.

The impact of the Americans, though, was always far greater than their actual numbers. They were different, "men, women and children of other race than ever was there before," wrote the American Irene Wright. "A hard-headed, strong-handed, dominant and domineering people who refer to all things not American in a tone which tells the truth: they have made the native an alien in his own land."[7]

A few months before the Hay-Quesada Treaty was due to come to a vote in 1905, some of these strong-handed settlers decided to act. Down with ratification, up with the Stars and Stripes! On a balmy November day, more than a hundred American residents of the Isle of Pines rallied at Pearcy's hotel in Nueva Gerona and issued a declaration of independence from Cuba. Isle of Pines Mayor Juan Manuel Sánchez, former major in the Liberation Army and a personal bodyguard of General Antonio Maceo, ordered the Rural Guard to defend all public buildings. Demanding recognition by and protection from Washington, the mutineers seethed with a defiance duly reported in the local press. From Havana, U.S. Ambassador George Squiers supported them and was soon retired for his lack of tact.

One account had it that bloodshed was averted only because the waterworks, consisting of a goat cart carrying a large water jar, ran away and everyone was reduced to stronger drink.[8] Before the hour set for the declaration of war, Cubans and Americans had reached a state of sentimental good humor that prevailed until they all dispersed peacefully.

"A rebellion well-timed to influence the Senate at its next session, but not calculated to win popular support in this country," wrote the *New York Globe*. The *Baltimore American* was outraged: "The Cuban Government will probably arrest the ringleaders of this little mutiny and put them in jail.... A few months' imprisonment would calm the ardor of these empire-builders and divert their energies into more useful channels. If they don't like Cuba it is easy enough to get away from there without involving the American Government in their prejudices."

Charges against the ringleaders were dismissed, and they continued their mischief. In September 1906, during the "little war" over election frauds in Cuba, Sánchez got wind that the American Federation, a paramilitary settlers' group, was hiding weapons for an armed uprising backed by Cuban supporters on the Isle. He ordered his men to search Pearcy's hotel, Koritsky's general store, and several other American-owned establishments. The search produced little except the ire of Federation Secretary Charles Raynard, who protested to Sánchez and to U.S. Secretary of State Elihu Root.

The Hay-Quesada Treaty, which all this action was designed to defeat, didn't even reach the Senate floor that year. The United States sent troops to Cuba to end the "little war" and extended its second occupation from 1906 to 1909, under Provisional Governor Charles E. Magoon.

Cuba had $13 million in the national treasury when Magoon took over the government. When he left in 1909, there was a deficit of $12 million.[9] Some of the money was spent on building roads, upwards of $175,000 on the Isle of Pines alone for the "Cartroads of Magoon . . . wide avenues, carefully graded and finished with extensive drains and cement culverts where needed. Few rural communities in the United States are supplied with ways for traffic as good as these."[10]

The American provisional government also commissioned U.S. Army agent G. R. Fortescue to search for a sheltered deepwater harbor on the Isle of Pines. The Fortescue mission found no ready-made solution, but in 1910 engineers began construction of an 1,800-foot dock on Siguanea Bay at the mouth of Los Indios River. The project was designed to accommodate coasting freighters and fruit steamers drawing no more than fifteen feet of water, for the loading and direct shipment of produce to U.S. and Caribbean ports. It was expected to reduce export costs and speed deliveries by eliminating double handling, fees, and delays in the overcrowded port of Havana. However, the project was never completed, and the idea lay dormant for the next eighty years.

Meanwhile, Edward J. Pearcy filed suit to force clarification of the smaller island's status and move his smokes into a competitive market. Pearcy grew tobacco and manufactured cigars on the Isle of Pines, then shipped them through the port of New York for sale in the United States. The port collector seized Pearcy's cigars under the Dingley Act for the imposition of duties on articles imported from foreign countries. Pearcy sued to recover their value, asserting that the Isle of Pines was a part of the United States and hence domestic territory free of import taxes.

In *Pearcy v. Stranahan* the Supreme Court ruled on April 8, 1907, that Cuba, historically and politically, included the Isle of Pines; that the official acts of the Spanish government, from 1774 to 1898, treated the Isle of Pines as part of the political division known as Cuba; and that its status had not changed since then. The Dingley Act did, indeed, apply. The Court then cited the opinion Secretary of State Elihu Root had given to an American resident of the Isle, Raynard, following the disturbances of the previous year: "The treaty now pending before the Senate, if approved by that body, will relinquish all claim of the United States to the Isle of Pines. In my judgment, the United States has no substantial claim to the Isle of Pines. The treaty merely accords to Cuba what is hers in accordance with international law and justice."

The decision effectively ended the growing of tobacco as a commercial crop on the Isle of Pines. Duty-free entry to the U.S. market was the cutting edge for competition with Cuba's famous *vuelta abajo* leaf grown in Pinar del Río Province.

Other products, though, had already found a competitive niche in the U.S. market. Captain J. A. Miller was modestly successful with his own Smooth Cayennes and other pineapples grown on the Isle of

Pines. In 1912 he sold 170 crates: 60 from his own orchards, 92 from the McKinley Fruit Growers' Association, and the rest from individual growers. Miller personally supervised the shipping of this top-quality fruit and invited others to the packing house to observe the value of "a good uniform pack."[11] Grapefruit, cultivated with advice from the Florida Department of Agriculture, was the top export crop. In the best of these early years, American growers shipped nearly 300,000 crates of what everyone recognized as the sweetest and juiciest grapefruit in the world, while oranges, tomatoes, peppers, eggplant, cucumbers, and melons from the Isle also tempted U.S. palates.[12]

Neither the Supreme Court decision nor the secretary of state's opinion on the status of the Isle dampened the ardor of eager American settlers who continued to stake out their orchards and farms, build their homes, and sell their duly taxed merchandise in the stubborn belief that the Isle of Pines was or would one day be American.

The new American townships were named McKinley, Columbia, Westport, and San Francisco Heights; or they retained the old names of Santa Fé, Las Piedras, Santa Rosalia, Santa Barbara, and La Cañada. The settlers erected their own bungalow-style dwellings using native pine supplied by local sawmills that operated near the settlements. Unskilled construction labor was readily available among the native islanders, but for farming and domestic work the Americans preferred Jamaicans and Caymanians, mainly because they spoke English.

The Isle of Pines Bank, established in 1905 with James A. Hill as secretary, acquired stocks and public funds to be used for infrastructural development (roads, telegraph, telephone), made loans, and set up other companies as necessary. One of these was the Isle of Pines Steamship Company, created in 1908 with William J. Mills as secretary-administrator and later owner.[13] This successful enterprise remained in the Mills family until 1956.

In 1915 the newly founded Isle of Pines Ice and Electric Company promised to construct an electric plant that would "provide services to the entire population" and also to build an ice plant. Seven years later, the commercial "exploitation of a telephone network on the Isle of Pines" was initiated through the Farmers and Growers Cooperative Telephone Exchange.[14]

While they planted and built, the settlers evolved their own closely knit society. Social life centered around the American Club in Nueva Gerona. Members—there were more than a hundred in 1910—were welcome to drop by the clubhouse any time to read the newspapers or write a letter. They also enjoyed the community dances held there and sometimes brought the family or friends in for a meal.

"Horseback is the inhabitant's favorite means of transportation, and riders can be seen everywhere," a visitor wrote in 1910. "The native ponies are fine for riding and following trails," and as for "Autos—There are some fifteen on the island, ranging from the simple runabout up to the seeing-the-island car."[15]

The first of many special-interest groups was the Hibiscus Club, formed for literary purposes in 1905 by twelve American women living in and around Santa Fé. The members then opened a free library that soon became a permanent and well-supported community resource available to everyone. Pioneer, social, quiz, and bridge clubs followed, as well as businessmen's, growers,' and commercial associations.

Since the citrus orchards required years of expensive cultivation before they became profitable, an owner might have to hire out as a part-time carpenter or mason to tide him over. He might also lease part of his land to sharecroppers for a specified percentage of the profits. In the case of the smaller and less affluent settlers, the head of a family might work stateside half the year and spend the winter months farming or doing odd jobs on the Isle.

The settlers had their own churches (Episcopal, Methodist, Presbyterian), schools, stores, and two American-trained doctors on call. They also had their own American cemetery, a shady rural park with flowers planted at the foot of granite tombstones. Burials began there in 1907. There were family plots with impressive markers, like the one belonging to the wealthy Pearcys. The more modest Koenig plot recorded family deaths over a forty-year period, beginning with J. M. Koenig in 1942, and ending with Stefania Koenig in 1981.

THE NORTH OF THE ISLAND

In 1909 German-born John and Hermine Koenig came to the Isle from Cleveland, Ohio, with their three American-born children: Edith, John, and five-year-old Harry. Gertrude, William, and Paul were born on the Isle. Of the six, only Willy and Harry stayed. Harry died in 1995, the last American on the Isle.

Harry Koenig (1904–1995)

My parents were German immigrants who became American citizens. My father worked as an electrician there in Cleveland and went to night school to learn English. The climate wasn't very good, though, and he had a lot of trouble with colds and flu. The wind comes down from Canada and crosses the Great Lakes, and it's awfully damp in Cleveland—real cold, too. I guess he must have read some advertisement for the island because there were lots at the time. You know, "Go to the Isle of Pines, and you can plant grapefruit and sit on the porch. You don't have to work no more!"

So my father bought the property up there from one of the land agents they had at the time, and we come here in 1909, when I was five, and lived on a farm he bought out in Santa Barbara. In the beginning, he used to go back in the summer and work in the States. He always got his job again when he went back. He'd work there for six months or so, then come down here for the winter. Three of us was born up there and the three

youngest down here. My brother Willy was born in Santa Bar-
bara, and he still lives out there. He's Cuban. I'm the last of the
Americans.

We grew fruit and vegetables, mostly for ourselves, and my fa-
ther would do electrical and engineering jobs that came up. We
went to an American school. All the schools out in the country
were American in those days, with American teachers. The Span-
ish I picked up afterward, here and there, and I learned German
from my parents because they used to speak German together.
When we weren't in school or working on the farm, we'd go fish-
ing or swimming. We grew up next to a river, and we used to
spend most of our time in the river, so we were all good swim-
mers.

I was too young for World War I, only fourteen, but I remem-
ber some of our American neighbors went off to fight. After that
war, quite a few families came here from Europe, from Poland
and Russia and the Ukraine. Most went to the States first, and
from there they came down here. I guess they thought life would
be easier down here than up there. Some of them stayed here,
too, like the Racheks. They live out in the country there near
where Willy lives. I was married twice, and both my wives were
Ukrainian. My second wife, Stefania, died just a few years back,
right after I fell and broke my hip.

Vasily Rachek

I was born in the Ukraine when that part of it was Polish. My
parents went to Europe and then, after World War I, they went
to the States and came to Cuba from there. My father worked
for the Electric Company in Havana before we came to the Isle,
and my brother Ramón was born here. We had a good farm here.
We raised cattle and grew almost everything we ate.

There were lots of foreigners here before, and they all lived in
language groups. We knew English, so we got to know all the En-

glish-speaking people. It was after the 1926 hurricane that most of the foreigners left. Those with money travel. Those without stay. Others came later, but they weren't so wealthy.

I married a Cuban from Oriente Province, and we had a daughter. After 1959, I worked for three or four years out there in what's now Granma Province as head of machinery. That job was more than I could take: work day and night, too much responsibility. Then I got divorced and came back home. Ramón and I thought of leaving in the late sixties, but when mother got sick, we stayed to take care of her. She died in 1982. There didn't seem to be any reason to leave then. We've been here all our lives.

The government built this big reservoir here, and it ruined my land. Nothing will grow now. I should be recompensed, but I don't bother. Our farm is small. We keep cows and chickens and grow some things for the house like pineapple, melon. We get by. If you smoke or drink, you look for work. I don't do either. We sell the heifers to the government. They pay most for one- or two-year-olds, then fatten them for slaughter.

We live way in from the road and don't go anywhere except to visit a neighbor. One of us always stays in the house, though, so nobody steals the farm livestock and equipment.

The Koenigs and Racheks were atypical families in two ways: the parents were naturalized, rather than native-born, citizens of the United States, unlike most of the other families who came to the Isle in the early years; and, unlike other American farmer-settlers, they planted truck gardens to supply the family table rather than fruit orchards for commercial production. Importation of food products that could easily be grown on the Isle was common under the Crown, too, when cattle ranching was the main commercial activity.

In Nueva Gerona, just a block from Las Casas River ferry terminal, was a wooden bungalow set among trees and flower beds that looked more like New England than the tropics. Built in 1929, it differed from the modern tile-roofed brick and cement structures in the neighborhood and also from the few older wooden houses with columned porches. On the corner across from the bungalow, which belonged to the Sundstroms, is the sprawling single-story house where Andrés Fernández has lived since his father built it in 1912. Father and son helped construct the Sundstrom bungalow, too, but it was a Sundstrom who designed it in a style so different from the rest of the architecture in this Cuban-Spanish frontier town.

Edith Sundstrom lived there happily for most of her adult life until, in 1987, she left the Isle to visit Miami and never came back. For nearly ten years after her departure, the bungalow was kept as she had left it, and many of her neighbors believed it should be turned into a museum. Edith always remained as American as her house and friends. She had the blonde good looks of her Swedish American parents, spoke English with a Boston accent, and never learned Spanish because she had no reason to.

Edith Larson Sundstrom, in Miami

We came in 1920 and I'll tell you, my first year on the island I was one pretty lonesome gal. You see, I was fourteen years old. I was born in Fitchburg, outside Boston, but we had been living in Hartford, Connecticut, for four years and a little bit more, because my father, Oskar Larson, found good work there. I was just beginning to get out and have a good time. I was going to church, the Swedish Lutheran church. I was in with the church work. I loved Hartford, and I had a boyfriend I liked a lot.

My mother, Astrid Maria Larson, had a brother who had gone to the Isle of Pines, and he kept writing letters about how good it was down there. Besides, mother was sickly, and dad thought the milder climate would be better for her. She lived to be ninety-five, you know. She died on the Isle in 1978.

We went from Massachusetts down to Tampa, Florida, by car. My aunt and uncle came with us. Then we couldn't get the car over, so we left it there and came on by boat. It took us a year before we got our car.

We lived on a farm near my bachelor uncle's place, about six miles out of Nueva Gerona in what they called Santa Ana. My uncle had a horse and wagon, and we bought a buggy. That's how we got around that first year. We all lived on separate farms out there, some distance apart.

My uncle grew vegetables: peppers, cucumbers, and, later, tomatoes. My father, when he came to the island, was a pretty husky man, and he got as skinny as a rail plowing and planting. Never worked so hard in his life. And the crop was a complete disaster. We were absolutely broke until he got a job managing a citrus plantation.

After a while, I got to know people, and people invited me places. We went to beach parties, and there were dances at the club and different things. Life began to change. In the third year Albert came, and life was wonderful after that. His two older brothers had come down earlier, and my family had known them in the States. Albert was thirteen years older than me, but you wouldn't know it; in fact, later on he looked younger than I did.

Now this is kind of silly, but I fell in love with him the minute I saw him, and that was his first night on the island. He and his two brothers and his sister-in-law were at my aunt and uncle's place. My aunt played the piano. One of Albert's brothers played the violin, and the other played drums. I was sitting in the car listening to them play, and Albert came out and said, "Come on, let's dance." So we went up on the porch and danced while they played. And that was the beginning.

We used to go to the Methodist church in Gerona because there wasn't any Lutheran church on the Isle when we first came. Later there was one—not Swedish Lutheran, but Lutheran—and of course there was the Catholic church and other denominations.

I didn't finish school. They didn't have the facilities when we came. In later years, yes, we had an American school, a very fine high school; but then I was half grown up.

There were doctors, Cuban doctors, and they had a good reputation. Cuban doctors are good. Occasionally we had to send somebody to Havana for attention or hospitalization. We had a small, small hospital then. When I left, there was a big, big hospital.

All the people we knew were English speaking, and most were Americans. I would say 90 percent of the people we knew were Americans. But there were always all kinds of people on the island: lots and lots of Japanese, some Chinese (there were several Chinese stores in town and they were always well stocked); then there were Jamaicans and people from Cayman who spoke English.

THE SOUTH COAST

Cocodrilo, on the south coast of the Isle of Pines, is now less than an hour's drive over a two-lane dirt and hardtop road from the checkpoint at the edge of Lanier Swamp. While the Americans were settling the northern part of the island in the early days of the twentieth century, Cayman islanders were settling the south coast they had discovered while fishing for turtles. Descendants of British planters and Jamaican slaves, they are a mulatto people, sun-bronzed and strong. Many, like Maud Jackson and Dick Hydes, have blue eyes.

Bertha Maud Tatum Jackson

I was born in 1898, and I came here with my parents when I was six years old. We came from Cayman Chica in a little boat, not a motorboat but a sailboat. There were my two older sisters, and I was the smallest, the youngest of the family. My father was Tamper Tatum and my mother Edwina. We lived down at Coco-

drilo Point, where all the ones that came from Cayman Chica lived. Down there, the men would go turtle fishing at Siguanea Bay and sell the turtles in Jamaica.

My husband, Moddriel Jackson, was one of Atkin Jackson's sons. The Jackson family came from Grand Cayman and they all lived up this way. The Jacksons were the first ones to settle here, and they bought the land, so that's why it was called Jacksonville, though it was always Cocodrilo on the map. Cocodrilo Point was way down there where the fishery is now. In those days, Jacksonville and Cocodrilo Point, they didn't have to do with each other, so I didn't know my future husband when I was little.

We were married in the Lutheran church here. I'll show you the certificate. It's so old, but you can read it: "William Moddriel Jackson, of Caleta Grande, Isle of Pines, and Bertha Maud Tatum, of Caleta Grande, Isle of Pines, married the 9th of October, 1915."

View from the caves at Punta del Este

I miss my husband. He was always good to me. There was just him and me in the house after the chillun all grew up. I had eight. One died when she was a baby. She had whooping cough. All the chillun here had it at that time, and it even hit me because I never had it before. But she died.

We raised all the others in this house that Moddriel built in 1923. It's built of plaster, lime, and wooden boards, and I believe it's still strong because all the posts is in the ground.

My husband used to be in charge of the land here. You know they cut a lot of wood here, and the boats would come in and load it, and he was the one to see after the loading and how much the men got paid. Then he and the others worked in fruit on the other side of the island. Moddriel had his boat, too, but he was getting paid for checking up on the works and the likes of that here.

He had a little boat called La Paloma *that used to traffic up and down the coast, carrying people from here to Gerona and back. After we married, I would go with him because we had friends, a Cuban family, here, and she was like a sister. If I went to Gerona, she would take care of my chillun, and if she went some place, I would take care of hers. That's how we always lived.*

There was no road here then. It was this government that put the road through so you can go by bus to Gerona. So we would go on La Paloma. *She wasn't such a big boat but she was nice. Moddriel was a good boatman. All the women here trusted him because he knew how to sail. Later he put a motor in the boat, but it didn't work very well, so he took it to the garage in Gerona to see if they could fix it. The garage caught fire, so that was the end of the motor and the boat too.*

Dick Hydes

*I came here in 1905, when I was a few months old, so they tell
me. My father was William Hydes, and my mother was Elizabeth Jackson, but we didn't come with the first Jacksons because
we didn't have enough money there in Grand Cayman.*

*What my father told me was that Atkin Jackson bought some
of the land from an American who owned the whole place here,
point to point. It was good timber land, very good timber land.
Atkin Jackson knew a lot of people who wanted to come but
didn't know how to get the land. Well, he was a good fisherman
and boatman, and he used to come to Gerona, too, so he found
out who owned the land, which was a man named Pearcy in
Gerona.*

*Yes, the land was bought from Pearcy. He had a land company
that came down from the north. And Atkin Jackson did the nego-
tiations with Hill, a man by the name of Hill, who was president
of the bank. Fifty acres was all Jackson could get because nobody
had much money; and the company didn't want to sell much of
the front land either, because later it would bring a good price. So
every one of the neighbors took a piece. I think my father owned
about seven acres. All who came knew about the land from Atkin
Jackson before they got here. He told them so they could come.*

*Atkin was the father of Moddriel Jackson, who died a few
years ago here. Atkin had three sons and two daughters, and he
was the one who started this community. That's why they used
to call it Jacksonville.*

*My father helped cut the wood for the big wholesalers of tim-
ber, and worked in the fruit business. I worked in the sawmill.
The land was full of pines and all kinds of trees. It was beautiful,
beautiful.*

During the winter months especially, American tourists augmented the resident population on the Isle. Some were patients who stayed for weeks, even months, to take treatment at the mineral waters. The Santa Rita Springs Hotel was opened a stone's throw away from the ruins of the nineteenth-century hotel where Samuel Hazard had stayed. *Terry's Guide* for 1926 recommended the new hotel as "modern, American, clean, comfortable . . . known for its good food and charm. Rates from $5 a day."

A flagstone path led from the hotel under a giant laurel directly to the springs. Nearby was a tennis court and golf course. Guests could hire autos or saddle horses for country trips and transfer to the steamer at the Júcaro River landing. Motor launches waited there to take visitors fishing or sightseeing along the coast.

The Isle of Pines Steamship Company ferried the tourists between Batabanó, on the south coast of Havana, and the ports of Júcaro and Nueva Gerona, for $8 one way ($10 with stateroom berth) or $31.50 for an all-inclusive two nights on the water and two full days and a night on the island. Captain William J. Mills, general manager of the steamship line and a financial power in many island enterprises, lived in one of the beautiful tropical homes of Santa Barbara, where visitors were lodged at the pleasant Santa Barbara Inn.

The package tour included Nueva Gerona (marble quarries, caves, and mineral waters), the Santa Fé medicinal springs, and nearby Jones's Jungle, whose owners personally guided tourists through the luxuriant botanical garden they had cultivated. Growing alongside a horseshoe-shaped stream were all sixty varieties of hardwood found on the Isle of Pines and many from other regions as well. Rare trees bearing fruit on their trunks or dangling pods from long tendrils; huge ponderosa lemon and tall Brazil nut trees; a riotous profusion of flowers and blooming shrubs; gaudy parrots, sober thrushes, and tiny hummingbirds vibrating everywhere made this the showplace of the Isle of Pines and all of Cuba for more than a quarter of a century.

Cuban crocodile bred on the Isle

The island's early history as a pirates' haven also led to enticing rumors of buried treasure and insistent attempts by travel writers to identify it as the island described in Robert Louis Stevenson's *Treasure Island*.[16] Sunken ships off the coast testify to that early history, but the real treasure throughout the twentieth century was always the Isle's golden grapefruit. The fruit was sanctified by Cuban bartenders in the classic cocktails invented during the 1920s; the Isle of Pines, an ever popular cooler, is composed of two ounces of grapefruit juice and an ounce and a half of light rum stirred over cracked ice.

SNATCHED FROM THE PLATTER

The most vocal annexationist on the Isle of Pines in the first quarter of the twentieth century was a veteran of the Spanish-American War named E. de Laureal Slevin, who had fought under Colonel Leonard Wood in the famous Rough Riders regiment organized by Lieutenant Theodore Roosevelt.[17] As editor of the influential *Isle of Pines Appeal* from 1922 to 1925, Slevin vociferously supported U.S. ownership of the Isle in a campaign that reached its climax in the Thanksgiving supplement of 1924.

Covering the entire front page was a caricature, in color, of a grinning Uncle Sam recognizable by his striped pants and starred vest. A platter on his outstretched arms held a plump roasted turkey labeled Isle of Pines. The caption read: "For the bright prospect that this will come to pass before the year is out, we are profoundly grateful to divine providence and to our country on this Thanksgiving 1924."

On an inside page, the weekly printed a photo of Harriet Wheeler, well-known island ceramist, taken at a luncheon in her honor before she departed on an important mission: "Mrs. Harriet Powell Wheeler left on Tuesday's boat for Cuba, to proceed thence to Washington, where she will complete the task undertaken last year of defeating the Hay-Quesada Treaty, which would in violation of the promise of our government to the American pioneers who settled the Isle of Pines and of the American Constitution, transfer this bit of American territory to Cuba under the specious plan of giving it in consideration of the grant of lands to the United States for naval stations. A host of friends went to the wharf to wish Mrs. Wheeler bon voyage."

It was a steamy time on the island. Aaron Koritsky was fined ten dollars for flying the American flag over his general store. Several other Americans, including Slevin, were jailed after they attacked Sanitation Department officials who fined them for violating local hygiene laws.[18] To assert their pro-Cuban sentiments, some of the islanders organized a patriotic meeting at La Favorita Hotel, in the center of Nueva Gerona. At that first meeting, they set up a Pro–Isle of Pines Defense Column and named as its chairman civic leader Enrique Bayo Soto, an uncle of Andrés Fernández on his mother's side. Conferences, meetings, and cultural activities were organized by the Pro–Isle of Pines Patriotic Committee. The vanguard of this Havana-based pro-ratification movement was the Anti-Imperialist League of the Americas, headed by the charismatic University of Havana student leader Julio Antonio Mella, also a founder of the first Communist Party of Cuba.

In Washington, Cosme de la Torriente y Peraza presented his credentials as Cuba's ambassador to the government of Calvin Coolidge. His primary goal was to ensure that two-thirds of the U.S. Senate voted in favor of the Hay-Quesada Treaty. Harriet Wheeler, representing Americans on the Isle of Pines, brought the Senate an appeal against ratification signed by 100,000 women.

At this late date Torriente had the backing of bankers and investors such as J. P. Morgan and Company, whose larger commercial interests in Cuba were in no way jeopardized by recognizing the legality of Cuba's claim to the Isle of Pines. Their influence on senators was considerable. On the other hand, Harriet Wheeler's sincere appeal was directed to the senators less concerned with high finances, and Torriente had to reach them, too.

In his memoirs, Torriente referred to a discussion he had with a Republican opposition senator who controlled a significant bloc of votes. The senator told the ambassador he would vote against ratification unless Torriente could prove to him that Cubans on the Isle of Pines had taken part in the War of Independence. "That was easy," wrote Torriente, "I showed him the volume of *Mi Mando en Cuba* (My Mandate in Cuba) by General Valeriano Weyler, the much hated Spanish captain-general, containing his report of the conspiracy and revolutionary attempt on the Isle of Pines organized by Evangelina Cossio. The senator thanked me and told me he was certain any just man would support my cause, as indeed would he."[19] Whether or not that was the deciding argument, the Hay-Quesada Treaty was finally ratified on March 13, 1925, twenty-one years after it was signed.

For Mella and other young firebrands, the ratification was a long overdue recognition of Cuban sovereignty—and no thanks were due Uncle Sam. Most Cubans, though, reacted with jubilation and gratification, and President Alfredo Zayas organized a mass rally of thanks. Mella interrupted it with a flaming anti-imperialist speech that got him arrested for public offense. In the national elections that followed later that year, Zayas was replaced by Gerardo Machado, who promised a popular program of administrative honesty, public works, and reduction of the public debt.[20]

A week after the treaty was ratified, E. de Laureal Slevin published his resignation statement: "The Isle of Pines is Cuban now . . . and Americans wishing to remain on the island will have to adjust themselves to that fact. They ought to be able to get along with their Cuban friends, at least until they can get away."

Those who stayed did have to adjust, and finding a scapegoat for the situation seemed to help some. "I couldn't believe it," Edith Sundstrom recalled years later. "The men said that if they had sent a male delegation, everything would have been different. Of course, when we heard the treaty had been signed and the Isle was turned over to Cuba, it was heartbreaking news because we had always thought it was going to be American territory. But how could those men blame Harriet Wheeler?"

THE BIG BLOW

American residency on the Isle was successively reduced by drought and storms that destroyed fledgling orchards, the call to military service in World War I, and the economic crash in 1920.[21] In 1921, the U.S. congressional farm bloc pushed through legislation to protect domestic fruit and vegetables from foreign competition, which forced Isle of Pines farmers to look for new markets or leave. When the U.S. Senate finally ratified the island as Cuban in 1925, more Americans went home.

Harriet Wheeler was not among them. Undaunted by politicians or chauvinists, she stayed on the island she had adopted as her home, quietly potting and glazing. She was driven out by a more awesome and devastating foe: the hurricane of 1926, which demolished her house and kiln, forcing her to depart—temporarily—for the States. It was the worst storm of the century. Earlier hurricanes in 1907, 1915, and 1917 had damaged crops and buildings as they swept across the island, but the storm of 1926 hit everywhere.

Andrés Fernández, in town

> Barbaro! *It started around eleven at night and went on until five the next morning. The hurricane of 1917 was terrible, too, but it only lasted half an hour. The one in October 1926 wreaked havoc and it went on for hours. We tried to make it to the Gómez place because that was the safest house in Nueva Gerona, but there*

Nueva Gerona parish church, single-steepled since 1926 hurricane

wasn't time. The wind was so strong it knocked off one of the steeples on Los Dolores Church. We got back home and battened down as best we could. The storm tore open the door, ripped off shutters, lifted part of the roof, and threw debris everywhere. My mother's head was cut. My little brother was hit in the face by a flying rock that broke two teeth. There he was bleeding and crying, and we couldn't leave the house with him until around 4:30 A.M., when the wind began to calm down a little.

The destruction was terrible, vegetation burned off and buildings collapsed; lots of dead animals because no animal can stand up against that wind. The hills were stripped, just stripped. Recovery took a long time. A big ship came from Guantánamo Base, with a pile of sailors on it. The ship couldn't get in the harbor, so everything had to be transferred to launches. They brought rice, coffee, bread—everything—and they stayed for a few days to help us. They were quartered at the Anderson hotel, all of them dressed in white because they were sailors; and they distributed the food from the Gómez house.

Maud Jackson, on the south coast

I was in this house with my seven chilluns, and Moddriel wasn't here. He was over with the fruit pickers, and I was alone with all the little ones. Lydia, my youngest, was only a year old. My father-in-law, Atkin Jackson, wouldn't leave me in the house. He wanted us to be where it was safer. So we went over to a hotel that had been turned into a school, to wait until the storm passed. The building had a zinc roof, and when the storm hit, the roof blew off in pieces. It looked like planes flying across. We had to run out of there, and we got back home.

The people came from all over to our house because Moddriel had built it strong; at that time, it was the strongest house here. Finally there were twenty-six people in this little living room. Well, the storm took off the porch that had been parted in two to make a room for the girls. *Except for that, the house wasn't damaged and nothing happened to any of us.*

Out in Júcaro, Mosako Harada, recently arrived from Japan, was working as a day laborer with other Japanese farm hands and saving his pennies to buy land for himself. His recollection of the 1926 hurricane remained clear years later.

Mosako Harada, on the farm

That hurricane was some experience. It flooded the fields and tumbled all the houses, because the houses of the Japanese were made of wood, like most of the Cubans'. Caballero, everything, absolutely everything was destroyed!

At that time, I was working for a Japanese farm owner named Yamanashi. It was my first year here, my second in Cuba. The agent in Japan had arranged a three-months contract for me to work in Santa Clara. The agent did everything. I think I paid about thirty dollars, and he took care of the passport, the transportation, and the contract. I went directly to Santa Clara, where I would be able to earn fourteen or fifteen pesos a week after my contract was up, or so the agent told me. That sounded like a lot of money to a twenty-year-old who was earning twenty-five cents a day—but it was all lies. In Santa Clara, the banks were folding, the stores were closing, and I was one of thousands who couldn't find a job.

That's when I heard there were some Japanese farmers on the Isle of Pines who sold their products in New York and were doing pretty well. That's how I happened to come here in 1926.

The hurricane that year was a lesson. I didn't lose anything because I didn't own anything then. But once I did, I first built a garage to protect the equipment—tractor, truck, van, and tools—and a barn to shelter the animals. Then I built this concrete house, strong and safe. I've gone through four hurricanes since 1926, and I haven't lost anything.

Poet Hart Crane (1899–1932) was broke and desperate when he decided to spend the summer of 1926 at the home of his maternal grandmother, Elizabeth Belden Hart, on the Isle of Pines. He remembered the house only dimly; he didn't even know housekeeper Sarah Simpson, who would attend to his needs; and he had all but forgotten the beautiful beaches, marble mountains, and luscious homegrown grapefruit he had described to friends in Cleveland after his first visit to the Isle twelve years earlier.

Crane needed a retreat where he could get on with his ambitious poem *The Bridge*. The boat trip down and living expenses there would cost him much less than he'd need to go somewhere else, or even to stay in a stifling New York apartment. On the Isle, he'd be far away from the personal jealousies and financial worries that were eating into his creative efforts.

He arrived at Villa Casas in May and found it run-down but spacious, just right for his work. Mrs. Simpson turned out to be cheerful, tolerant, and completely sympathetic to Crane's capricious moods. She soon became his dear Aunt Sally. The other members of the household were Attaboy, the loud-mouthed parrot; Pythagoras, a baby owl; and the unwanted mosquitoes.

Crane hacked out the dead orange trees in the front yard and planted royal palms in their place, enjoying the tough exercise and tasting the abundant fruit that grew everywhere. Citrus was the only thing not in season, and he enjoyed all the others: avocados, breadfruit, guavas, limes, kumquats, cashew apples, coconuts, bananas, papayas, tamarinds, pomegranates, and, best of all, mangoes. He sent letters to all his friends about them and even wrote a poem called "The Mango Tree."

Purged physically and spiritually, he turned to *The Bridge*. Soon he was engulfed in the project, writing day and night with all his faculties keyed to making it "divine." In the third week of October, however,

Crane was moved by a divinity he had never before known, when a hurricane whirled through the island, animating him as nothing else had done.

When the storm began, Crane rushed to meet its exigencies by dragging the yard furniture and tools into the house, slamming and bolting wooden shutters, and positioning pots under leaks in the roof.[22] As the wind battered the house, flaking plaster from ceilings and walls, Mrs. Simpson grabbed Attaboy and the other household pets and took refuge under the biggest bed, where Crane joined them. There, with the wind shaking the entire house, poet and housekeeper told each other tall tales of all their wild moments, punctuated by gales of laughter. When the wind slackened from time to time, Hart crawled out to bring food and drink and place Victrola and records within easy reach. On one venture outside to relieve natural necessities, a fierce gust of wind stripped him naked. As Mrs. Simpson wrote him later, "The picture of Adonis striding through the tall grass garbed *a la natural* . . . makes me wonder how we both came out so well."

It was a memorable hurricane high that continued with a dance to survival the morning after the storm, when, balancing cushions on their heads, Hart and Mrs. Simpson swirled through "Valencia" and one-stepped out to clean up debris. To top it off, a contingent of sailors from the USS *Milwaukee* reached town the following day, bringing enough rescue food and drink for all. Back in New York, Crane wrote a poem filled with more somber images of that hurricane:

ETERNITY
"September—remember;
October—all over."—Barbadian Adage

After it was over, though still gusting balefully,
The old woman and I foraged some drier clothes
And left the house, or what was left of it;
Parts of the roof reached Yucatan, I suppose.

She almost—even then—got blown across lots
At the base of the mountain. But the town, the town!

Whores in the streets and Chinamen up and down
With arms in slings, plaster strewn dense with tiles,
And Cuban doctors, troopers, trucks, loose hens . . .
The only building not sagging on its knees,
Fernández Hotel, was requisitioned into pens
For cotted Negroes, bandaged to be taken
To Havana on the first boat through. They groaned.
But was there a boat? By the wharf's old site you saw
Two docks unsandwiched, split sixty feet apart
And a funnel high and dry up near the park
Where a frantic peacock rummaged amid heaped cans
No one seemed to be able to get a spark
From the world outside, but some rumor blew
That Havana, not to mention poor Batabanó,
Was halfway under water with fires
For some hours since—all wireless down
Of course, there too.

                              Back at the erstwhile house
We shoveled and sweated; watched the ogre sun
Blister the mountain, stripped now, bare of palm
Everything gone—or strewn in riddled grace—
Long tropic roots high in the air, like lace.
And somebody's mule steamed, swaying right by the pump,
Good God! As though his sinking carcass there
Were death predestined! You held your nose already
Along the roads, begging for buzzards, vultures
The mule stumbled, staggered. I somehow couldn't budge
To lift a stick for pity of his stupor.

For I

Remember still that strange gratuity of horses—
One ours, and one, a stranger, creeping up with dawn
Out of the bamboo brake through howling, sheeted light
When the storm was dying. And Sarah saw them, too—
Sobbed. Yes, now—it's almost over. For they know;
The weather's in their noses. There's Don
But that one, white—I can't account for him!
And true, he stood
Like a vast phantom maned by all the memoried night
Of rain—Eternity!

Yet water, water!

I beat the dazed mule toward the road. He got that far
And fell dead or dying, but it didn't much matter.
The morrow's dawn was dense with carrion hazes
Sliding everywhere. Bodies were rushed into graves
Without ceremony, while hammers pattered in town.
The roads were being cleared, injured brought in
And treated, it seemed. In due time
The President sent down a battleship that baked
Something like two thousand loaves on the way.
Doctors shot ahead from the deck in planes.
The fever was checked. I stood a long time in Mack's talking
New York with the gobs, Guantánamo, Norfolk—
Drinking Bacardi and talking U.S.A.

Hart Crane

Harry Koenig

*In 1926, after the big hurricane, the American boats came from
Guantánamo Base to see if we needed any help here. My little
brother Paul saw the sailors in town here all dressed up in their
white uniforms. He decided he wanted to be a sailor. He said
when he was of age he was going to go and be a sailor, an
American sailor. So when he got to be seventeen, he went to the
States and signed up with the Navy because he thought they
were going to put him on a boat and then he'd see the world. Instead of that, they made him a swimming instructor in North
Carolina; then they put him on a tugboat in San Diego. He never
got outside the country at all during World War II. But he stayed
up there at the end of the war.*

*The first time I went back to the States was after that hurri-
cane, the one in 1926. There was a three-mast schooner out here
in the river, and the storm put it up on the beach down here a
little ways, and a couple of Americans came down and bought it.
They wanted to take it off the beach and do business. I asked
them if they'd take me up to the States, and they said, "Sure."*

*We went up to Mobile, Alabama, on the boat. That was back in
the depression, you know, and practically every day there'd be
freighters come in that didn't go out again because there was no
work. They found out then there was no business, so they let the
boat go. I stayed there a couple of months in Mobile, and then I
went up to Princeton, Kentucky. I worked there a little. Then my
father wrote me and told me to come back again. So I went to
Tampa, because there was a ferry that used to go to Havana
from Key West and Tampa. Then from Havana, I went to
Batabanó and came back on the* Pinero.

My oldest brother worked on the Pinero. *After the hurricane,
why, the steamship company went up to the States and bought*

the Pinero, *and it had diesel motors in it. They didn't have no one to run the motors because all the other boats before that were run with steam. Practically all of them burned wood. But my brother knew about diesel motors because he had gone to Camagüey, where my sister was living, and got a job there on a tugboat with a diesel motor. He worked along the north coast there for six years. There were lots of places where they had to take the sugar out in barges, you know, because the big boats couldn't come in.*

Then he came back to the Isle, and he was loafing around the place when he got the job on the Pinero, *which was owned by Robert Mills. Mills lived out there in Santa Barbara. His father, the captain, lived in the house before you get to the tunnel of trees, and Robert lived on the right side after you get to the end of the tunnel.*

After the hurricane of 1926, the Isle remained trapped in a long tunnel of depression that undermined socioeconomic life for the next quarter of a century. Once again, as in colonial times, it became a neglected geo-economic space of Havana, but for someone like Harry, who had grown up on the Isle, it was a whole lot more viable than Alabama or Kentucky, or even Camagüey.

2 The Long Depression

In the first quarter of the twentieth century, the Isle of Pines had a remarkably low incidence of crime, most of it petty and property-related. Theft of food or farm tools, damage to farm lands by stray animals, and drunken brawls were the main offenses, in that order.[1] Both foreign and native residents figured as plaintiffs, defendants, and witnesses. On the whole, it was a peaceable and innocent time, and certainly the most prosperous in the history of this generally neglected territory.

The image of the Isle changed in the gloomy shadow of the Presidio Modelo, twin of the Model Prison in Joliet, Illinois, begun in 1923. The plan of circular cell blocks with a central guard post was conceived by British prison reformer Jeremy Bentham (1748–1832) to control prisoners while providing light and air lacking in the dungeons of his time. In the twentieth century, the design was as outmoded as the choice of an island venue. The location of a huge penitentiary to hold common (and occasionally political) male prisoners from all over Cuba on the Isle of Pines reinforced its past history as an isolated penal colony. More pragmatically, however, the Presidio Modelo, run by the military with state funding and prison labor, would generate local services and provide graft for high-level officers at a time when most of the juice had been extracted from the commercial orchards.

Cuban President Gerardo Machado laid the cornerstone in February 1926. The prisoners assigned to build it finished the first of four circular tiered buildings in 1928. They were quartered there while completing the ten-unit complex with capacity for 5,000 prisoners. Total cost, estimated from various budgets, was 2 million pesos—using local materials and unpaid labor.

While the enormous fortress was going up, the resident population was growing, and its composition was changing. As the Americans departed, new immigrants came from the Cayman Islands and Jamaica to join turn-of-the-century arrivals and their prolific offspring in the search for jobs. Most old-timers stayed on the south coast as fishermen, lumbermen, and charcoal makers, but many younger people moved to the northern part of the island and worked the abandoned orchards as squatters; or, if they were lucky, hired out as farm hands and domestics with lodgings and meals included.

When Harriet Wheeler returned to the island in 1928, she brought two Canadian farm hands, the Jordine brothers, to work her land in Santa Barbara. That same year, she also hired a young Jamaican named Augustus (Gus) Forrest, who had impressed her favorably when she met him shortly after he came to the Isle in 1924. The following year, Sylvia Baker, an attractive twenty-four-year-old Jamaican woman, arrived in Nueva Gerona and soon joined Harriet Wheeler's extended English-speaking family.

Model Prison, opened in 1930, deactivated in 1967

Sylvia Adina Baker Forrest (1905–1996)

My father was a black Jamaican, and my mother was white—
her mother was from India, and her father was Scots, born in Ja-
maica. I wanted to look like my mother, but she always said her
brown children had softer skin. We lived pretty well while I was
growing up. I went to school and even studied piano. But times
were bad when I left Jamaica. First I went to Cayman and stayed
there for nine months, but that wasn't any better. So, in 1929, I
came by boat to this island. I didn't know any Spanish. I thought
everybody spoke English, so I looked for English-speaking people
when I came.

I met Gus at the dance hall. I wore my red dress and, oh, I
looked swell! I told Gus, "Mon, I like you." He had on a gray suit
and a white shirt and a nice pair of shoes; and he could dance!
He was three years older than me and had been married before,
but she wasn't around. He looked mighty good to me: real hand-
some, yes, and how he could dance! His voice was good, too. He

had a good voice to sing. We danced fox trot, waltz, round dance, calypso, everything. Gus was violinist at the Church of God. I was raised a Baptist, but here I went to the Church of God. I was working in town, for the judge. I had my own room and a piano that my neighbor in Gerona gave me with all her music books.

Gus was working for Mrs. Wheeler. It was Gus who told me about Mrs. Wheeler and Mrs. Wheeler about me. I was at the judge's when I hear a knock-knock, and I open the door and see a big, smiling American woman, and she says, "Are you Sylvia?"

And I say, "Why yes I am."

"My boys told me you were looking for work," she says, "and I wonder if you would like to work for me."

"I wouldn't mind," I said, "because I don't like it in town. I'm from the country, and I love to stay in the country."

Fifteen years I worked with Harriet Wheeler, until she died. I did all the cooking, baking, everything. I couldn't find a better home. She called me daughter and made no distinction with her own. She had two daughters, and one of them, Vera, was married to an American named Edward Pearcy and they lived here for many years. He looked after everything, the land and all that.

Mrs. Wheeler gave me this Victrola for my birthday. I loved it, but I didn't want to take it, and I said "Oh, no." When she insisted, I asked her why.

"Because you're a good girl," she told me.

Look at it, made in 1906 by the Victor Talking Machine Company of Camden, New Jersey. I want to give it to a museum. You know, it's history. It's like Edith Sundstrom's house.

Mrs. Wheeler was an artist and a teacher. I used to watch her make pottery, and she always explained what she was doing. Well, I went to my room one night with some clay, a board, and a fork. When I showed this vase to Mrs. Wheeler the next morning she said, "When did you do it? It's wonderful." I've sold everything else I did, except this. I won't part with it.

Out this way, we were all English-speaking, mainly Jamaicans and Caimaneros. We all helped build the Four Corners School, and that's where we had the dances. The school isn't there anymore, but it stayed open through most of the forties.

When I came, you didn't mix much. The Cubans, que va mix! But now everybody mixes. When I saw how strict the Cuban men were with their girls, "Oh my," I say, "yes, these are real people." You know, the girls weren't allowed out alone. They had to be with their mama or an older sister or brother. Now it's all changed, too much, too much. They had some good, nice girls here, well kept. That was in 1929, but it went on that way for many years.

We all lived with Mrs. Wheeler in her big house: the Jordine brothers and Gus and me. After she died, we stayed on. The men took care of the land and the crops, and I worked in the house. We lived that way until the government built the reservoir in the sixties, and the water flooded the house and all the land. We were recompensed. The government built a house for the Jordine brothers and this one for Gus and me. And after Gus was killed in the field, well, they gave me a pension of eighty-five pesos a month. That's what I live on. And I have lots of friends. I live by friends.

Sylvia's best and closest friends for the last forty years of her life were her down-the-road neighbors Anne and Rulle Ebanks, both born on the Isle, children of Cayman Islanders who came to the south coast and moved north to farm during the depression years.

Rulle Ebanks (1923–1991)

I was born on the south coast. That's where my parents went first when they came from Cayman. Most of the people down there came from Grand Cayman in those days, and they came because the fishing was good: lots of fish, lots of turtles. They built their own houses with lumber felled in the forest there, built them on posts so they were dry. They all spoke English. We never spoke Spanish. I have two sisters and three brothers who were born here too, but they went back in the sixties. I stayed because I had one son, my oldest son, who was in service and, you know, we didn't want to leave him. When that one was out, the next one was in, and we never did want to leave them, so we stayed here.

Well, my parents moved up here when I was seven, and my father started farming. He worked for an American who had a big farm, where I worked too. The American had a stroke, so we took care of him in his house and worked his farm. When he died, we stayed, and that farm was ours. I started buying my own land as soon as I could, but that farm was where I grew up.

I met Gus at dances. Then, after Annie and I got married, we moved up here, and Gus and I started farming together. I was with him when the truck tipped over and crushed him to death. Since then I've been trying to help Sylvia.

We used to sell some of our farm produce in Havana and some to the stores here, and we did direct orders from the farm for customers who came by. Now we just keep a garden for ourselves. This area used to be full of fruit trees and farm land, but they built the dam, and the whole place flooded. Water came right up to the windows of our house. They built us a new house, but about ten acres of land were lost. This little island has more dams than anything else. The bulldozer just came in one day and knocked down all the fruit trees, and the soil was ruined. You can't farm here now. They paid us compensation, but the orchards are gone forever. They said more water was needed for irrigation, but everything was irrigated before. Now, with a much bigger population, they need more water, but they also need more land for growing.

Anne Yates Ebanks

Like Sylvia says, we've all been friends for many years. I was born not far from here, near where Sylvia and Gus lived with Mrs. Wheeler. My mother and father came from Cayman to the south coast, then moved up here. When my father died, my mother went back to Cayman and died there at the age of ninety-six in 1986. I have one sister in Cayman, and I have another sister and a brother on the south coast.

It was only after Rulle and I were married that I began to learn a little Spanish. I couldn't go to school because it was too far and there was no transportation. So the little schooling I got was from an old lady, Miss Elly. She used to keep class, you know, for a few of us. She was Cayman also, so we learned in English.

In our family, we all worked together. I had ten children, but I always milked the cows, took care of the garden and the kids; and from the time they were little tots, our children had their tareas, *their jobs. Our parents were that way. When I was small, I helped my mother with her weaving. She used to weave straw baskets and rugs and sell them, and I used to do that too. I don't sell much now, though. You have to take out a license, and I can't afford to do that just to make a few baskets—because I only do weaving when I don't have any other work to do. The materials are from the plants that grow around here, so I still make baskets by order. But I don't make them any more to sell on the street. That's not legal.*

We always worked hard, and we had a good time, too, especially dancing. We used to have community dances, and we had private parties, too. We danced every weekend. All the English dances—sucu-sucu, round, waltz, polka, and so on—came from Cayman. Sucu-sucu[2] is really the round dance, but the Cubans didn't know what to call it, so they gave it that name from the sound: all the houses on the south coast are made of wood, and the feet moving across the floor boards made that sound, sucu-sucu.

Sometimes Sonny Boy would play. We all grew up together, so it was like a family fiesta. He had his own group of musicians from the Isle, and they played all that traditional music they learned from their parents. In those days Sonny Boy wasn't so well known off the island, but he was very popular here. Now he's usually booked up at the clubs in Varadero, for the tourists, you know. The young people today don't have any use for that kind of music. They like rock and all the new sounds.

Mongo Rives, founder of *sucu-suco* quintet Tumbita Criolla

The sucu-suco *was created here on the Isle by native* pineros, orientales, gallegos, *and maybe African slaves had something to do with it, too. So all these people together, with their idiosyncrasies and their isolation, created a new rhythm that wasn't a* son montuno *or a* guaracha *but something different. It began evolving in the last century, because my great-grandmother told my father how they did it then, when they called it* rumba *or* rumbita. *Then, around 1910, people here began calling it* cotunto, *but, by the twenties, all those names had disappeared in favor of* sucu-suco. *Because, at that time, lots of Americans were coming to Cuba and especially to the Isle—their project was to grab the Isle—and they heard this music they called* suc-suc *from the sound the dancers made. Pretty soon it became* sucu-suco, *and that seems to be the official name, though some pronounce it* sucu-sucu.

And it is totally pinero. *It has nothing to do with* caimaneros, *who have their own musical forms from Cayman, Jamaica, England—that Sonny Boy knows much better than I do. And when we're together, Sonny Boy says, "I'm going to talk about my* music, and Mongo Rives can talk about his music, which is the sucu-suco." That way we're in agreement, because Sonny Boy is a very good musician, and he is my friend.

From the twenties through the forties, my father had a sucu-suco group called El Retardao, because they came late to the peasant fiestas. But they also stayed late; they were in no hurry to leave. Then I took over from him with my own quintet, which expanded to nineteen after the triumph of the revolution; but in the nineties, we couldn't make ends meet with such a big group, so now we're seven. Our instruments are accordion, bongo drums, guitar, marimba, tres, machete (played by our vocalist Rosa González), and lute, which is my instrument, though I play them all. Our main line is sucu-suco, but we also play montuno, guajiro, merengue, bolero—all the traditional music.

While Mongo Rives and Sonny Boy were playing their respective types of traditional music, Rulle and Gus were working the orchards and farms laid out and planted for commercial harvesting by American entrepreneurs. With the departure of the Americans and the deepening of the depression, farming became a family enterprise that, with hard work, could provide a continuing livelihood. However, there were no more managerial farm jobs available for the likes of Albert Sundstrom. He was looking for other work, but it took a couple of accidents to get him settled in town.

Edith Larson Sundstrom

One day in 1929, Albert was visiting the sawmill that a friend of his owned. While they were talking, Albert happened to put his right hand down on the whirring saw behind him and cut off four fingers. After the hand healed, he learned to write and do almost everything else with the stubs of those fingers, but at the time, he even wanted to cancel our wedding: "You're not going to marry a cripple," he said. That was rubbish, of course. But he had a hard time for awhile.

He used to come into town to get his hand dressed. After he finished at the doctor's, he'd walk around town a little, and he almost always stopped in at Aaron Koritsky's hardware store, or I should say, general store, because the merchandise ran from tools to apples that Aaron shipped in. Aaron was one of those good Jews, a generous person and friendly with his customers. He and Albert enjoyed sitting down in the store to chew the rag. One day Albert asked him, "Aaron, do you know how much stock you have in this store? Do you ever take an inventory or anything?"

Aaron said he couldn't be bothered with that, but he must have thought it over, because a couple of days later when Albert dropped by, Aaron said he was going up to Boston to see his family and he'd like Albert to keep an eye on the business while he was gone. "Maybe you could do an inventory," the old man said slyly.

About a month later, as he was finishing up the inventory, Albert got a telegram that said: "Meet me in Havana," and was signed "Koritsky." At the designated hotel, Albert was met by Aaron's brother with the news that Aaron had died of a heart attack in Boston. Could Albert help him straighten out Aaron's affairs on the island? The two of them came over together and Koritsky looked at Albert's inventory, inspected the store, and offered Albert the business. "I'm not interested in this at all," he told Albert. "I'll sell it to you for a song."

So that's how Albert happened to get the hardware store. We were married right after that, in the Nueva Gerona courtroom, and we had our reception at Upton's Restaurant. Then we moved into the two rooms we had fixed up in the back of the store, one as a bedroom and the other as a kind of dining room/kitchen with lots of chairs.

We had been married only a short time when Albert decided to take out Cuban citizenship. Although he was Swedish born and had lived in the States, he didn't want to go back to either country. "I have to belong somewhere," he said, "and this is home to me." Albert was really part of Gerona. He had friends and friends; everybody loved him. He even became mayor once for three months. Now wasn't that an honor?

Most evenings after we locked up the store, we'd take a little walk. That's how we found an empty lot just a half block from the river, where we decided to build our home. Albert's brother Gunner supervised the building. We had a neighbor across the street who was a first-class carpenter. He and his son did most of the construction and interior finishing, and Albert put his two cents' worth in wherever he could.

We moved into our little cottage three years after we were married and lived there all those years. It was a wonderful home, and our garden was beautiful. We had a fireplace, too, and sometimes it was chilly enough to light a fire.

One cold evening shortly after we moved in, we were sitting in front of the fire when there was a knock on the door; and there was Peggy Rice with her husband and the two boys. They had just rented a place in Gerona and had heard that we were Americans living in town.

I shut my eyes and see Peggy the way she looked that night. She had a tam-o'-shanter on her head and a sweater over her shoulders and her eyes were as bright as our welcome fire.

"You're the first people we've been able to talk English with," *she laughed. It was the beginning of a long, long friendship.*

Margaret Pitman Rice (1901–1992)

British-born, like her late husband, Maurice, and their elder son, Derek, Peggy remembered their move to Canada in 1922 as the beginning of the adventures she described in her unpublished diary, *My*

Life So Far, written at age seventy-six when she was laid up with a broken hip. She started those memoirs with a nostalgic stanza so familiar to her that she didn't bother to put it in quotes or attribute it to Robert Browning:

Grow old along with me
The best is yet to be.
The last of life, for which the first was made.
What I aspired to be,
And was not, comforts me.

It was the first note of resignation in the life of this adventurous woman, always ready for whatever came along. At eighteen, during World War I, Peggy was keen on her job as a government file clerk and excited by war-torn London. She marveled at a German Zeppelin aflame in the London sky "like a huge cigar . . . a wonderful sight until you thought of the poor boys burning up with it, even though they were the enemy."

Married to Maurice in 1919, Peggy gave birth to Derek the following year, and the three soon left for prosperous Canada to join Peggy's sister and brother-in-law. Maurice had been a radio operator during World War I and quickly found a good position in a Toronto radio company. After Peggy gave birth to their second son, Harry, the young couple moved out of Peggy's sister's place into their own. They had a good life in Canada until 1929, when the depression hit and Maurice's firm went bankrupt. There were no jobs to be found. Maurice's hobby of tinkering with fine instruments and old watches supplemented what he got on the dole, but it wasn't enough to feed a family of four.

Peggy Rice, from her diary

One day Maurice was looking at a very old turret-wound watch.
He had the casing apart and discovered, much to his surprise, a
piece of paper pressed in the lining. On it in fine writing—he had

to get a magnifying glass to read it—was a description of treasure buried on an island in the Pacific, giving all the details of its location. Maurice checked a lithographer, a lawyer, the owner of the watch, the local newspaper. Everybody agreed it was genuine and it was ours.

Imagine the excitement in a family with two young boys. After the newspaper story, we had letters from people offering to help us finance the trip to find the treasure. So we sold our furniture and, with the help of an enthusiastic backer, bought a boat called Casaco and sailed from St. Johns, Nova Scotia, down the east coast to Miami. From there we crossed the Gulf Stream, where we were curious about the change in the color of the sea. It was a deep blue and very beautiful. We entered Havana harbor, passed the famous Morro Castle and dropped anchor almost opposite the British consulate.

We left Havana a few days later and sailed along the north coast of Cuba, around the western tip and into the Caribbean, heading for the Panama Canal. That's where the trouble began. Our boat started leaking so badly that my husband had to send out an SOS. As we furiously bailed out water, we saw a gunboat and attracted it toward us by using a small mirror. Captain Braulo Fernández helped us in every way he could and towed the Casaco to the prison dock on the Isle of Pines, where we were viewed by many curious American, English, and Cuban people.

While we were waiting for the boat to be fixed, we rented an apartment in Nueva Gerona. That's when I met Edith Sundstrom. She was the first friend I made on the island.

The repairs were more than we could afford, so we sold the boat and rented a small house in a grapefruit grove. We were very happy. The boys made lots of friends with the young people in the surrounding houses, all different nationalities of English-speaking people: American, Swedish, Hungarian, English. We had lots of surprise parties where everyone would bring some food and the young people would play games and dance; no hard liquor or beer, just soft drinks or juice. I look back and think what fun those youngsters had dancing to music from an old record player, swimming, horseback riding—they all had horses—and playing games. There was no television or movies.

I became pregnant again. I was thirty-eight years old. The midwife at the little maternity hospital in Gerona told me I was rather old to start a young family and, with my permission, she would take care of the matter for me. I thanked her and said I wanted my baby. I hoped it would be a girl so my boys would have a sister. They took good care of me in the hospital, and Joan was born on September 13, 1939, without any problems. I was very lucky to have an abundance of milk. I was able to feed three babies: my own and two others. Later, when I would meet those two youngsters in town, they always greeted me with much affection, as if there was a bond between us. Joan grew into a lovely baby. The young girls adored her and were always making playsuits, panties, and dresses for her. Of course, I knew the attraction wasn't only Joan. Remember, I had two good-looking lads. After all, the girls had to have an excuse to be always at our house.

As time went on, the boys wanted spending money. Although my husband had work, the salary in those days, especially here, was very small. We had to pay their tuition at the American School, the rent, and food. We had very little left over for clothes. So the boys were able to get work during the fruit-packing season, and, for an eight-hour day, the wage was $1.25. That was a fortune to them and made them feel very independent as they could buy their own clothes and shoes and other things.

There isn't much to say about Maurice. My husband was a woman-chaser. He was very intelligent, except about sex; and I wasn't sexy. On the island he took to lots of women and lots of drink. Then I discovered that the treasure map was a hoax. That *was such a blow to me. I couldn't imagine anyone could do something so awful. It was a complete swindle and, of course, he could never go back to Canada. I hope he is forgiven for his sins. I can't forgive him!*

Separated from the other islanders by language and culture, the Japanese immigrants toiled in the fields and maintained their own customs. Like the English-speaking settlers, many of them never learned Spanish, or learned only enough to sell their cucumbers, melons, and tomatoes. In those days, the majority were single men, contracted into poverty and working hard to survive.

Mosako Harada, farm and family

During my first three years on the island, I saved almost everything I earned so I could buy a farm of my own. Yamanashi sold me one of his three farms, and I've been working for myself ever since. After three years alone here, I wanted a family. I wanted to marry a Japanese, a good woman, and have my Japanese family here. I talked to my friend Julio, as one Japanese to another, and he said he'd have his younger sister come marry me. He wrote his father, and his father agreed that a friend of Julio's would be a good match for his daughter. So we exchanged papers and made a contract, and the father sent his daughter Kesano to marry me. That was in 1929.

Kesano was twenty years old and had never been anywhere. She traveled alone by boat from Japan to Panama, and I went over to meet her. We were married in Panama because the papers were all in order. We took the boat to Havana, where I bought her a Singer sewing machine. Then we came to the island. Our first son was born in 1930, and we named him Julio after her brother.

Times were bad, bad, bad, especially from 1935 to 1940. We had to work day and night to feed the children, and they kept

coming one after the other until we had six by 1942. Kesano al-
ways worked more than anyone. Even when she was pregnant,
she worked in the field: one day in the house, one day in the
field.

I had melons, sweet potatoes, peppers, tomatoes—all beauti-
ful—and I couldn't sell them. You had to pay for shipping, and
local products had preference in Havana. Then there was a
drought and after that lots of rain. We gave the stuff away and
some just rotted.

THE POLITICS OF PRISON

As the depression deepened, the Isle became less and less attractive to
new immigrants. Between 1919 and 1931, the population more than
doubled, to a total of 9,450, then leveled off and hovered around
10,000 until the end of the 1950s. The 1931 census was the first to
include 2,659 common prisoners residing in the Presidio Modelo.
Between September 1931 and May 1933, when his dictatorship was
overthrown, Machado also sent 539 political opponents to the new
National Men's Prison. While the men were confined in the Presidio,
11 women convicted in Havana of demonstrating against Machado
were sent to the Nueva Gerona prison in the old Cavalry Garrison.
Other opponents were forced into exile, among them Evangelina
Cossio, who returned to Cuba after Machado's fall.

In numbers, diversity, and militancy, the men represented a challenge to authority even behind bars. At the same time, they had the
unofficial status of prisoners of war in time of peace. Thus they were
separated from the common prisoners and treated with the deference
due the enemy. They could read, converse, and organize their free
time as they liked, as long as they stayed in line. This separation and
preferred treatment later became law and was generally respected.

The imprisoned radicals of the 1930s—among them Raúl Roa, who
served as Cuba's dynamic and polemic foreign minister in the 1960s

and 1970s, and Puerto Rican–born Pablo de la Torriente Brau, the militant writer killed in 1936 while fighting on the republican side of the Spanish Civil War—assuaged the "bitter hours of prison," as Roa called them, by reading, writing, conversing, and dreaming away their impatience.

Although they weren't personally abused, the political radicals were agonizingly aware of conditions around them. Pablo de la Torriente Brau later denounced them graphically in *La Isla de los 500 Asesinatos* and *Presidio Modelo:* "Thousands of screams, cries of dying men drowning in the mud and putrefying matter of the swamps; cut down by the sabers of the soldiers; shot down like fleeing deer; dying of starvation, cold, and thirst in the cells; treacherously strangled in the circular cellblocks by older inmates; hurled like rag dolls from the top floors to crumple on the pavement; put to sleep forever on the operating table by an injection, with the terrified or accessory silence of the nurses. . . ."

The incidence of "criminal injuries" rose briskly on the Isle of Pines, and 90 percent of the cases originated inside the prison, where Warden Pedro A. Castells ruled with abusive tyranny. The guards, many assigned to the prison for violations of army or national police regulations, frequently incited, extorted, and tortured prisoners, inflicting concussions, broken limbs, and knife and gun wounds that maimed or killed their unarmed victims. Some deaths were covered by the *ley de fuga*, shooting prisoners in the back for "attempted escape." Physically damaged and morally degraded, the inmates resorted to drugs, rape, murder, and suicide:

MODEL PRISON MONOLOGUE OF DEATH

Now you live in a niche in the side of a giant steel and concrete hole. Your niche with a barred window that looks outward and an open space that faces the hole. Beatings, screams of dread and anguish from prisoners held captive by simple bars of iron.

They keep the light on so they can always see your every move.

Remember, Antonio? You killed a man in your home town a year ago.

Knowing he would be drunk when he came, you hid, machete in hand, and waited.

Like someone trying to fell a big tree with a single blow, you swung the machete as he passed. You had to struggle to wrench the blade from his body.

You ran headlong to the river, stripped, and frantically tried to wash away the stains in the clean, clear water.

You never knew how they found out that you killed Pedro; they convicted you for murder.

Now you are in prison but it doesn't really matter to you because Pedro is dead and can never violate you again.

Not long ago, a fellow prisoner, one of many, just as big and strong as Pedro, and even looks like him, violated you the same way.

You are so weak, Antonio. You were born in hunger; hunger consumed your mother and has been like a sister to you ever since. That, Antonio, is why you have to wash the other prisoners' drawers and let them have their way with you.

In desperation, you creep to his cell, clutching your small, sharp knife, and plunge it into his heart while he sleeps.

But he has strength enough to get up and lift you into the air like a rag doll.

His eyes reflect death, his and yours. You feel the void of the hole, and I your scream crashing against the floor.

Juan Colina, Model Prison Museum Director, 1991 (trans. William Brent and Jane McManus)

Castells, it seems, was a prison tyrant who displayed compassion for the rest of humanity. Roa reported a case in point, when Castells kept the common prisoners outside during a hurricane with rain and winds so fierce that even areas of the prison were flooded.[3] After the storm abated and everyone was counted in and bedded down, Castells summoned the political prisoners to formation in the damp patio, where he reported, in a tremulous voice, the news of a terrible catastrophe: that same hurricane had wiped out the town of Santa Cruz del Sur, killing thousands of men, women, and children. Roa concluded that Castells deserved no less than a Freudian autopsy.[4]

Most folks outside the prison viewed Castells and his prison guards with tolerance and a certain degree of gratitude. Cruelty to faceless inmates was a minor flaw in a benevolent despot who distributed several hundred rations of prison food a day to poor families in the community. He also built and supported the Pedro A. Castells public primary school with funds siphoned from the prison. His guards, meanwhile, provided a stable clientele for the poor young prostitutes they picked up in a local bar while police and public health officials looked the other way. Only occasionally were charges brought against the woman, and often they didn't stick.

"Such cases," a state witness told the judge who had just dismissed a charge of prostitution, "require some action that will solve the problem of assistance for these women who hide their diseases out of fear and ignorance, and thereby represent a focus of infection that endangers the health of the community."[5]

After the fall of Machado, Castells was dismissed and later prosecuted (but never sentenced) for his crimes against the common prisoners. The political prisoners were released in time to rejoin the struggle that reached its zenith in one hundred days of revolutionary government controlled by the Students' Directorate, with the backing of the army rank and file, led by Sergeant Fulgencio Batista. As military court stenographer, Batista had listened to eight years of Machado's trials of revolutionary suspects, enough to turn him against the dictator while no doubt proving instructive for his own future.

The provisional president of this coalition government was Ramón Grau San Martín, a noted surgeon whom Machado had imprisoned on the Isle of Pines, but the moving force in his cabinet was twenty-six-year-old Secretary of the Interior Antonio Guiteras Holmes.[6]

Under pressure from workers and peasants who were striking and seizing property (mostly foreign-owned) and faced with U.S. threats of invasion, the civilian government was doomed to fall. Instead of invading, the U.S. acted as power broker for military stabilization under the leadership of Sergeant Batista. By 1934 most of the property confiscated from U.S. owners had been restored and a so-called reciprocal trade agreement guaranteed U.S. control of the Cuban market. Finally, the infamous Platt Amendment was abrogated.

In 1938 a new penal code was enacted, the first such revision since 1878. Called the Social Defense Code, it guaranteed prisoners certain rights and protection and removed prison operations from control by the military—until the army seized power in a coup headed by Batista, in 1952.

WORLD WAR II FROM INSIDE

In 1940 the Cuban Parliament adopted a progressive constitution that, among other stipulations, declared illegal and punishable all kinds of discrimination based on race, sex, class, or any other offense to human dignity.

Sworn to support the new Cuban constitution and loyal to his powerful northern benefactor, Batista was elected president of Cuba (1940–1944). In 1940 the United States was a passive supporter of the Allied forces battling the German-Italian axis, while Cuba maintained a strict neutrality. Then, on December 7, 1941, Japan attacked the U.S. military installation at Pearl Harbor, a stab in the back that catapulted the United States into World War II.

Two days later, Cuba issued its own official declaration of war, accompanied by a message from Batista stating that "the fate of the United States of North America in this conflict ... is our own fate." On December 19, following United States policy to the letter, the Cuban government declared a state of emergency and procedures for the internment of "enemy aliens"—a classification applied to all the male Japanese residents, some 70 percent of the Germans, and a little more than 50 percent of the Italians.[7]

Prejudice against Asians was nothing new in Cuba. After slavery was abolished, Chinese and later Japanese immigrants arrived as coolies, indentured servants, and contracted laborers at the bottom of the wage scale. During the depression it became convenient to push them out of the labor market altogether. In February 1935 an ardent minister of labor even suggested they be expelled from the country. With the attack on Pearl Harbor, the Japanese were specifically targeted for racial slurs.

At the first national Geography Congress held in Cuba in October 1942, Eduardo F. Lens y de Vera charged that "the government has contemplated with indifference the dangerous Japanese infiltration of the Isle of Pines in recent years." This "infiltration," the doctor warned, represented "a problem of the utmost gravity, because the dearth of a national population undermines the ability to assimilate foreign immigrants who conserve their own physiognomy, language and customs, constituting small nuclei that mirror the personality of each foreign country." By that time, those designated "enemy aliens" who were unable to pay the fee required to liberate them from that condition were safely behind bars, most of them in the National Men's Prison on the Isle of Pines, where 350 Japanese, 50 Germans, and 25 Italians were interned.[8]

Mosako Harada

A corporal from Squadron 43 of the Rural Guard came to pick us up. It was Wednesday, February 11, 1942, a little more than two months after war was declared against Japan. All the Japanese here got the same treatment. *The authorities told us the day before that they were going to take us to the Model Prison—just the farm owners, all men. They told us to be ready, that we had to go, and five soldiers came with the unarmed corporal in a truck. In all, they imprisoned 350 Japanese men—most of us lived here on the Isle—and some Germans and Italians were taken to another building.*

My wife, Kesano, was custodian of our few possessions and our six children. I remember that I made a sworn statement about the house and whatever else we had, as the law required.

Everything happened very fast that day. After they picked me up, they went to six other places. Ykio Minato came with us. He was married, too, and had a little farm in Santa Fé. The houses and properties of the bachelors were intervened directly—that is, a guard or government official was designated to take over without even consulting the owner.

The first months in prison were the worst—not because things were bad there. I was with my friends, all my neighbors, but there weren't any visits, and I didn't know how the family was making out. We had six children then, six before prison and six after. Ykio also had a family, wife and four children. We worried about how our wives were managing. All the others were single men who had no family visits and didn't know any Spanish.

Then came the first visit. We weren't allowed to be alone. The distance between us was at least ten feet, and we had to speak in Spanish. All the visits were like that. Kesano came with our littlest ones, and she brought fried fish and scallions. The prison food wasn't very good, and it certainly wasn't well prepared. We complained about it, but we heard later that other countries, like Russia, were much worse off than we were.

On various occasions, we asked for authorization to start a school, but we never got a response. Those who wanted to learn to read and write in Spanish had to find someone among our own group who was willing and able to teach. There was the same official indifference to our requests to learn trades, although we knew the prison had workshops and training programs.

We never learned why we weren't given uniforms like the other prisoners. Clothing was a problem that each prisoner had to solve as best he could. It was no secret that the Japanese authorities sent clothing and food through the International Red Cross, but not one shipment reached us or our families. Once they gave us a little bit of tea to share.

Minor medical problems were taken care of in the prison, with its few resources. When it was something a little more serious, the patient was treated by a private doctor in Nueva Gerona. For a really serious case, the only possibility was to take the patient to Havana, but there were always delays. One of the Japanese inmates died because of that.

On the whole, they treated us pretty well. First thing every day we had two hours outside the cell, walking around, and we could play games. But we spent three years there without doing any work. We had some books that the censor passed, and we taught each other Spanish, English, math, whatever we knew.

They let us out on December 20, 1945. When we came back to our land after three years in prison, the Cubans who were supposed to be taking care of the property for the single men refused to give it back. They demanded most of the harvest, the pigs, and they wouldn't move out of the houses that belonged to the Japanese. What a mess that was!

We were able to help our friends get back on their feet by providing fertilizer and pesticides, even land. My wife had been working like two, and I started working again. A couple of the older kids were able to help with the planting and harvesting. We planted more, we sold more, we bought more land, and market prices went up. *After 1945 we were able to sell all the melons and tomatoes we grew.*

Kesano Harada

I didn't know anything about farming when I came here from Japan. I grew up in the city, was the youngest in the family, and led a very sheltered life. My father arranged for my marriage to Mosako because my brother spoke well of him.

The family put me on the boat in Japan, and my husband-to-be met me in Panama. I had no fears about the trip. Everything was arranged, and it all seemed perfectly normal to me. I wanted to be a good wife, raise a big family, and help my husband in everything.

The hardest time was when he was in prison. All the men in the community were gone, and I had six young children to feed. I had to grow, and I had to sell. But I liked farming. My husband had taught me what and when to plant and how to cultivate. I grew melons, peppers, tomatoes, eggplants.

As harvest time drew closer, I had to guard my fields because somebody was always trying to steal the produce. I put out a scarecrow thinking a man's figure might keep the thieves away, but they knew it wasn't real. So some nights I slept in the field and moved around to startle the strangers. If I heard a noise, I flashed my lantern and they left. It was very tiring, but I made out. I grew enough to feed my children and sell the surplus to buy fertilizer and pesticides.

Lacking this kind of family vigilance, many of the single men had to sue to recover the property, farm tools, and harvest profits expropriated by members of the Rural Guard while they were incarcerated. On release the Japanese were offered family repatriation—and the loss of all rights and ownership in Cuba. Most of them, including

Harada, then became naturalized Cubans and continued to fight for the return of their possessions. Restoration for some came as late as 1954.

The traumatic experience affected the entire Japanese community collectively and in poignant individual examples: an attempted suicide by one of the men, who recovered with the help of psychiatric treatment; and a woman's incurable insanity, provoked by isolation and abandonment during her husband's imprisonment.[9]

WORLD WAR II FROM OUTSIDE

German U-boats hung off the coast of Cuba like frolicking dolphins. During World War II, the American naval attaché in Havana authorized writer Ernest Hemingway to hunt them along the north coast of the main island in his luxury yacht *Pilar,* disguised as a scientific expedition. Naval professionals dismissed Hemingway as a playboy and adventurer, while he made notes for his next novel *Islands in the Stream.*

Cuba's south coast was patrolled by a blimp, a submarine chaser, and motorboats stationed at the U.S. naval and air force base near Santa Fé on the Isle of Pines. All the Americans at the base knew Peggy Rice. To most she was mom, friend, and confidant who ran the recreation center.

Peggy's sons, eighteen and twenty years old, had gone to England to join the Royal Air Force. "It was awful when they left," she confessed. "I was glad I had little Joan." It helped, too, to support the war effort by knitting socks, caps, and sweaters for the United Victory Workers' Club. When the women asked her to be hostess at the recreation center they were setting up for the enlisted men, she was thrilled. She needed something to do, and she needed the money.

Peggy Rice

*The center was in the old Santa Fé church, which had a large
main hall with a raised platform that could be used as a stage.
On one side was a library with lots of wonderful books. We had
a billiard table, a jukebox, a piano, a big refrigerator, some chairs
and small tables, and plenty of space for dancing.*

*There was a grand opening night with ice cream and sand-
wiches on the house, beer and Coke for sale, and I was introduced as the hostess. After everybody left, we retired to our
small apartment at the back of the church, where we had managed to squeeze a single bed, Joan's crib, and a bureau into the
bedroom, leaving the couch in the living room/dining room for
my husband to sleep on.*

*In the middle of the night, I woke with a start to the sound of
wings flapping; and in the dim light, I could see black objects flying around the room and crashing against the window over my
bed. I awakened my husband, who I think would sleep through a
bomb attack, and we discovered our rooms had been invaded by
great big bats. Oh, how I hate bats! I was always told that they
were full of lice, and I was really frightened.*

*My husband got the bright idea that bats are attracted to light,
so he went outside with a lantern, and many of the bats followed. Not all though. I put a sheet across Joan's crib and sat up
all night. The next day we discovered their habitat in the eaves
and where they got in. We closed the hole and, using the lantern,
got rid of the rest of them that night. No more bats in the belfry
for us.*

*Our recreation center was very popular. The enlisted men
could come in during the afternoon to use the library, play bil-
liards, and listen to the jukebox. At night we showed movies, and
the people in Santa Fé could come see them, too. We set up about
a hundred chairs for movies and for the USO shows. We also*

had religious services every Sunday and sometimes during the week, both Protestant and Catholic.

Most of those boys had seen combat duty and thought it was great to be on the Isle of Pines. I tried to make them feel at home, and they called me "Mom." I would loan them my horse, Pinky, and they would have fun racing up and down the road. As a special treat, I'd sometimes make a fried chicken dinner with all the trimmings for a few of them. They would chase around and buy the chickens, pluck, and clean them. The girls who worked in our kitchen would fry them under my instructions while I baked the pies. The boys would invite their girlfriends, and we would have a nice feast before the center opened at eight o'clock.

Some evenings when the boys were tired of the jukebox and had some extra beer, they liked to sing. They might be homesick or they might be happy, but the singing made them mellow. I would thump out the old songs on the piano, and they really enjoyed that.

In her diary, Peggy listed some of the old songs they loved to sing: *Moonlight Becomes You, Good Night Sweetheart, I'm Always Chasing Rainbows, If You Knew Susie Like I Know Susie, Oh Susanna Don't You Cry for Me, Peg o' My Heart, Polly Wolly Doodle, When Irish Eyes Are Smiling, My Wild Irish Rose, Sweet Georgia Brown, My Blue Heaven, The Man I Love, Pack up Your Troubles, I've Been Working on the Railroad, The Sunshine of Your Smile, I Love My Baby, Old Shanty Town, I've Got Sixpence, Stardust, 'N' Everything.*

Although we sold beer (and it was cheap in those days: twenty cents a bottle), never once did any of the base boys take too much and make a nuisance of himself. They had the utmost respect for me, and they knew that if I saw a boy drinking too much, I would not sell him any more beer.

Once a month we had a dance, and the girls were brought from town with their mothers or aunts. They had to have a chaperon. The boys all turned up spick-and-span in their uniforms and behaved like perfect gentlemen. Many marriages came from these friendships. The Cuban girls are very pretty and full of laughter and friendliness. Not only the girls, but all Cubans; they are nice people.

I ran the center for three years. But, as they say, all good things come to an end. The center came to an end with the hurricane of 1944, the worst I ever experienced. The storm was coming for three days, with rain and hot, shifting breezes, before it finally struck on October 19. The poor old church was rocking on its foundations. Windows were blown in, the front door was blown open, and we couldn't get it closed. The wind was getting stronger by the minute. We decided it wasn't safe to stay in the building, so we gathered up food and water, cushions and blankets, and crawled in under the front steps. The space was like a small tunnel with enough headroom to sit up.

There were six of us, three sailor boys, my husband, Joan, and myself. We were quite comfortable out of the wind and rain, until I turned on my flashlight. There on the wall not twelve feet away was a huge centipede about a foot long, a horrible-looking thing. One of the boys said "Oh, my gosh," and I yelled "Eek!" and turned off the light. When I turned it on again, the creature was gone, and we all sat there on pins and needles wondering who he would bite first. But I guess Mr. Centipede was as frightened of us as we were of him because he just disappeared. When there was a lull in the storm, we all left for safer terrain.

The storm burned the leaves off all the trees, flowers, and shrubs and tore down houses. It looked like a wasteland. The center tilted lopsidedly, without windows or doors. Our outside shower room and toilet at the back of the building was upside down. And we were robbed; all the jars of guava jelly I had made and our dishes, clothes, even some furniture had been moved out. Everything that was left was sopping wet and covered with *leaves and sticks blown in from outside. So much destruction in one night! Yet within a week, new leaves and grass began to turn the landscape green once more, as if to say, "Nothing really happened, it was all a bad dream."*

BACK TO NORMAL

The hurricane of 1944 was almost as devastating as that of 1926. It hit the marble quarries—destroyed in 1926 and functioning again only since 1940 (with prison labor)—as well as the tile and brick industries; it washed out roads and farms, with a crop loss of 40 percent; it sank most of the boats moored in Las Casas River at Nueva Gerona; and it demolished many houses. It also damaged the Evangelina Cossio Primary School, inaugurated for the 1942–43 school year by Evangelina herself.

In the afterglow of a war fought to make the world safe for democracy, Batista retained his military rank but was succeeded in the presidency by his colleague from the thirties, Ramón Grau San Martín, who was elected in 1944 on the *Auténticos* ticket. Grau rode in on a wave of social promises—some of which he kept while also bleeding the national treasury in the style of Magoon. From 1944 to 1948, he raised wages, constructed roads and housing projects, started a rural school program, improved health facilities, and provided aid to the needy.

The Grau government recognized the Isle of Pines as a future tourist pole and began making plans for that eventuality by improving communications. At the end of 1945, the Cuban Telephone Company, controlled by the International Telephone and Telegraph Company,[10] extended international telephone service to the Isle of Pines, making it possible to call there from any part of the world and vice versa. At the same time, Grau committed what Andrés Fernández called "a real crime against history" by reducing the nineteenth-century cavalry garrison to rubble and building a school on the site. It could be argued that the Evangelina Cossio Primary School, finally located there in 1947, was a fair trade-off, but as Andrés and others commented, one of the few colonial landmarks on the Isle—which could have been a tourist attraction—was gone forever.

As postwar travel picked up, the tourists returned in ever larger numbers to Havana and Varadero and in trickles to the Isle of Pines. Travel guides followed, among them Sydney Clark's readable *All the Best in Cuba* (1946). In it Clark recounted (without mentioning Maurice Rice by name) the story of "a young man from Nova Scotia who was following a trail indicated by a mysterious chart (which he showed me) found in the back of a seaman's watch. It marked the spot—not on the Isle of Pines itself but on another key—where a quarter of a million dollars' worth of treasure was buried."

The "young man" had committed to memory the details of the location he had scratched off the chart and was slowly raising funds to finance his search, in which he expressed infinite faith. "He is still in Nueva Gerona, still full of faith, but the funds come slowly in that languishing town," Clark concluded. Maurice Rice never pulled off that hoax, and Peggy never forgave him for trying.

In his checklist of tourist sites on the Isle, Clark noted that the long-trumpeted arboretum known as Jones's Jungle had fallen on hard times for the oldest reason in the world: no money to keep it up. In contrast, he praised the mahogany and marble Model Prison as "a major sight of the island, indeed a major sight of Cuba . . . a remarkable affair physically and in its spirit and system."

Glowingly, Clark reported that none of the cells had doors, and the prison grounds were without walls or any other barriers; that the guards were unarmed trusties looking after 2,000 to 3,000 inmates; and that prison occupations included marble cutting, butchering, and barbering—all with sharp tools that could be, but never were, used as weapons.

Could this prison that Clark listed as "best in Cuba" be the same one a local civic leader and judge called a curse swallowing up the island? Waldo Medina, crusading lawyer, humanitarian, and follower of José Martí, was respected for his courage and honesty. On the Isle, he managed to survive the bullet fired by a latifundist who had tried unsuccessfully to bribe him into changing an adverse ruling, and he was known to be harsh on prison officials who embezzled public funds and extorted prisoners. Promoter of the airport and the first public library, Medina was a persistent and articulate critic of the "mastodonic, useless, and anachronistic penitentiary."[11]

For Medina, writing at the same time as Clark, it was "this lamentable deformity, along with geographic isolation—greater because of high shipping costs and the lack of economic, agricultural, and cultural incentives"—that had "reduced the Isle of Pines to a state of disaster and misery, with a diminished population that is economically stagnant and poorer than ever. It is an orphan with no moral resources or genuine citizenship."

The poorest and most marginalized residents of this orphaned island were the descendants of the black Cuban militiamen the Spanish Crown had repatriated from the United States in 1835 to colonize the Isle of Pines. A century later, their descendants still lived on the same rocky lands originally ceded to seventy-eight freed slaves, who retained the Spanish names of their former owners: Baca, Losaga, Zamorano, Zanco. Among those descendants was a great-great-granddaughter of the Baca family, who, looking back in the 1990s, recalled her childhood.

Virginia Baca Baca

My family are descendants of those the Spanish Crown brought from Florida to settle the colony of Reina Amalia in the last century. It was all virgin territory here, and their land was bad, but they had to survive. The lots they were given were triangular or angular and were divided among their survivors as inheritance. By the third generation, the lots were much smaller. Later some of them worked with the Americans who came to the Isle. But they always lived poor.

My father was José Baca, and my mother was Belén Baca, cousins. My great-grandfather, who lived until 1898, was named Villaverde. The Zamoranos, the Zancos, and other families were all part of Los Colonos. The little schoolhouse was built in 1925 and had a well where we got our water. We had to go to town to get sugar and salt, but we always had animals: pigs, chickens, a cow, a horse for transportation. The families worked the land together, with oxen. The houses were wooden shacks, and the bathrooms were the great outdoors. We bathed once in a while with a pitcher of water, and it wasn't until much later that we learned we were supposed to bathe every day. There was no electricity. If someone had a toothache, we pulled out the tooth with a string. Shoes were always the most difficult, and you had to wear shoes to school, so they had to last a long time. It was a hard life.

The little school built in 1925 was one of a dozen public and private primary schools on the Isle during the first fifty-eight years of the twentieth century. A boarding academy and a junior high school (both private) were the only secondary schools. In 1951 a public school to teach illiterate adults was founded, and the Model Prison had one teacher who was also the prison librarian. Public schools were dependent on budgetary whims and local contributions, private schools on tuition fees and occasional donations.

Private education arrived with the American settlers, whose children learned to read and write English from American teachers in American schools. Every American town on the Isle had its small school during the first quarter of the century. From 1935 to 1943, the English-speaking Antilleans financed their own primary school, Four Corners, in Santa Barbara (La Demajagua). In 1912 the Benedictine order opened a private junior high boarding school called St. Joseph's Academy, which later became San José Academy and was run by the Sisters of Charity, with the support of local residents.

In 1926 the American Central School was inaugurated in Nueva Gerona for children of the few remaining American families and Cubans interested in perfecting English. It was a private day school, financed mainly by tuition fees with occasional minimal grants from the Cuban government. All subjects were taught in English, and graduates received a ninth-grade diploma. When it opened, 66 percent of the students were American and white, but by 1956 the enrollment had become much more mixed. Of the 100 students, 47 were Cuban *pineros*, 25 were children of American immigrants, 25 were of Japanese parentage, 2 were of Chinese descent, and 1 was Hungarian.[12]

SEEDS OF DESTRUCTION

By the start of the fifties, Grau and his successor, Carlos Prío Socarrás (1948–1952), had so discredited the *Auténticos* with their excesses of violence, corruption, and public negligence that the party split. The younger, more radical members agreed with Eduardo Chibás's call for an ethical society through a new party, the *Ortodoxos*. One of the founders was university student leader Fidel Castro, who worked wholeheartedly for Chibás's election as president[13] and was himself a candidate for the Chamber of Deputies in 1952. At the same time, Castro created the party's radical action group (ARO) that favored insurrection.

Castro's choice of insurrection came naturally, out of Cuba's recent history and his own. His years at the University of Havana were filled with turbulent political conflict. He evaded several assassination attempts on and off campus as he rose to student leadership; attending a student meeting in Colombia, he fought in the street riots of the *bogotazo*; he was training on Cayo Confite, off Cuba's north coast, for an invasion of the Dominican Republic that would topple dictator Rafael Trujillo, when the Cuban navy arrived and arrested most of the expeditionaries. Castro managed to escape in a small boat.

Fidel Castro graduated from the University of Havana in 1950 with a law degree, a keen grasp of what political power was about, and personal experience with violence. He had a wife and a one-year-old son he could barely support, and he started his legal practice defending students, workers, and vegetable vendors who often couldn't pay him. Already a recognized orator and political figure, he was considered a shoo-in as deputy from Havana's poor neighborhoods in the June 1952 elections.

Those elections were never held. On March 10, 1952, Batista moved into Camp Columbia and, in a quiet, well-organized military coup, took over the country. Fidel Castro reacted with a broadside denouncing the takeover and a brief to the Court of Appeals demanding 100 years' imprisonment for Batista. He defended armed confrontation publicly and began to organize for it in secret.

On July 26, 1953, just sixteen months after the coup, Castro led the attack on Moncada Garrison in Santiago de Cuba and the barracks in nearby Bayamo. The action was a military disaster and a bloodbath; soldiers murdered 80 of the 135 rebel participants, many after they had surrendered. Only luck and public opinion spared Castro and those captured with him. Nevertheless, Moncada catapulted the still-unnamed movement and its leader to national fame.

The survivors were convicted of "crimes against the state powers" in the Provisional Court of Santiago and were given sentences ranging from seven months—for Haydée Santamaría and Melba Hernández, the two women participants—to fifteen years for Fidel Castro Ruz "as chiefly responsible."

Separated from the other survivors, Castro defended himself at a closed hearing. In prison, he wrote down that self-defense, which was smuggled out and printed as *History Will Absolve Me*, an exposure of festering social sores and a far-reaching program for healing them.

On October 13, 1953, twenty-four men who had been sanctioned to serve their time in Havana's Cabaña Fortress, near their families, were flown instead to the National Men's Prison on the Isle of Pines (the two women were held in the Women's Prison in Guanajay). The only prisoner who had any connections on the Isle of Pines was Jesús Montané, who had grown up there and attended the American school with Peggy's younger son, Harry Rice. Jesús's parents still lived in Nueva Gerona.

The new arrivals signed in and were photographed with their prison numbers. The photographer, a twenty-four-year-old *pinero* named Victor Hugo D'Alerta Soto, had inherited the job from his father, prison photographer in the thirties and forties, who had provided the testimonial photos for Pablo de la Torriente Brau's *La Isla de los 500 asesinatos*.

Montané was summoned back to photography the next day on the pretext that his mug shot hadn't come out and another had to be taken. The real reason was that his anxious parents had sent his uncle to see D'Alerta Soto and find out what was going on.

"Write your parents and give me the letter. I'll give it to your uncle later today," the photographer promised. So began the *Moncadistas* friendship with the official photographer of all the political prisoners in the Presidio between 1949 and 1959.

Fidel Castro arrived four days after the others and was reunited with his comrades in the prison hospital ward to which they were all assigned. With military action behind and ahead of them, the men used this space to prepare themselves. They turned the prison ward into a library and the fortress patio into an academy named for Abel Santamaría, Haydée's brother, who was tortured and murdered during the Moncada attack. Through the Nueva Gerona Amnesty Committee—headed by Sergio Montané and Zenaida Oropesa, Jesús's parents—and in personal letters to friends, they asked for books and more books. Relatives, lawyers, teachers, and intellectual sympathizers such as writer-agitator Raúl Roa supported their appeal, and they soon had more than 600 titles on philosophy, world history, political economy, mathematics, geography, and languages.

In a letter dated December 22, 1953,[14] Castro described how he crammed this educational wealth into the prison regime:

At 5 sharp, when you think you've just shut your eyes, a voice yells "Line up!" and we remember—if we forgot it while we slept—that we're in prison. The lights, left on all night, glare more harshly than ever; our heads feel heavier than lead; and we have to get up! Naturally, I spend less than 30 seconds putting on my shoes, pants and shirt: I won't sleep again until 11 at night, when sleep catches me reading Marx or Roland; or, as today, when I finish writing. To sum up, 5:30, breakfast; 8 to 10:30 a.m., classes; 10:45, lunch; 2 to 3 p.m., classes again; recreation until 4; 4:45, dinner; 7 to 8:15, classes in political economy and group reading; 9:30 p.m., silence. Every morning from 9:30 to 10, I explain philosophy or world history (alternate days). Cuban history, grammar, arithmetic, geography and English are taught by other comrades. At night, I teach political economy and, twice a week, public speaking or something like it. Method: instead of classes in political economy, I read to them for half an hour—a description of a battle, such as Napoleon Bonaparte's infantry attack on Hugomont, or an ideological topic such as Martí's plea to the Spanish Republic or something on that line. Immediately afterwards, several fellows chosen at random or volunteers talk for three minutes on the topic, in a contest with prizes awarded by the judges we have chosen. On all patriotic dates, we have special talks . . . on every 26th, a party; on every 27th, mourning with reflection and dissertations on the subject (on the days of mourning, naturally, there is no recreation or diversion of any kind).[15]

Castro devoured the philosophers, scientists, economists, political thinkers, and military strategists he captured in volume after volume. He read all the works of Martí and underlined what he considered most important. Nor did he neglect literature, from Shakespeare through Hugo, Dostoyevsky, and Somerset Maugham. He was particularly stimulated by Victor Hugo's *Les Misérables* and even more impressed by Karl Marx's treatment of the same topic in *The Eighteenth Brumaire of Louis Bonaparte*. Comparing Hugo's "purely romantic interpretation" with Marx's "scientific, realistic view of history," Castro observed: "For one, history is luck. For the other, it is a process governed by laws."

As he organized his fellow inmates, he also organized the amnesty campaign outside the prison through letters, secret messages, and instructions smuggled out, often in a match box with a false bottom. Always aware of the importance of propaganda, Castro sought exposure for his ideas in media articles and interviews whenever the opportunity presented itself.

One thing the men had not counted on was a direct confrontation with Batista while they were in prison. To their surprise, the general—in dress uniform and accompanied by a sizable group of officials—visited the prison on Saturday, February 12, 1954, to inaugurate a new power plant located some sixty yards from the hospital ward where they were housed. Once they learned of his presence practically outside their barred window, the men decided to greet the dictator. On cue from their fellow *Moncadista* and Isle of Pines prisoner Agustín Díaz Cartaya, they poured out the militant "Twenty-Sixth of July," an anthem he had composed denouncing "the evil that has plagued our troubled land, of errant, unwanted rulers and of cruel, insatiable tyrants." When the men concluded with a loud and jubilant "Long live the Revolution!" Batista exploded and left in a huff.

The general remained in a sour mood all through the ceremony honoring him as "an adopted and beloved son," during the banquet given in his honor by a local landowner, and even as he boarded his luxurious yacht three hours later to return to Batabanó, escorted by naval units.[16]

Reprisals came the next day. Five of the group were removed from the hospital ward and confined for two weeks in tiny isolation cells in the mental ward. Díaz Cartaya was beaten and left unconscious on the floor of his cell. The guards locked Castro in a larger fifteen-by-twenty-foot room across from the prison morgue, where he endured "the terrible humiliation of being engulfed in darkness" for forty days. After he got a light, books, and a hot plate, he was fairly comfortable. Although he invented ways of communicating with his men, he remained in solitary until they were all released from prison fourteen months later.

During that period, the prison authorities held outgoing mail and denied family visits in an effort to hush up the incident, but this caused mounting concern and insistence from relatives. Finally Sergio Montané and Juan Almeida, Sr., were admitted to see their sons and managed to talk to Castro for a few minutes before they were hustled out. Then, at the request of some of the students in Havana, Judge Waldo Medina used his knowledge and connections to penetrate the prison.

He and the students came on a Sunday (April 22, 1954), when prison warden Juan M. Capote wasn't there. That was fortuitous, since Capote hated Medina for sentencing his prison security guard to six months in jail for embezzlement and extortion. The acting warden treated the judge with deference; Medina could talk to Castro while the students visited the men in the ward.

Castro and Medina had never met, though they knew each other by name and reputation. With the prison official leaning against the cell door the whole time, they talked about Castro's health, his reading matter, the students, the weather. As Medina was about to leave, Castro observed: "So you're a judge in Havana now; well, they're going to kick you out for having come here."

Less than two years later, Medina was removed from his judgeship, but for more reasons than that visit: he had attacked the regime and prosecuted several of its corrupt officials. In the sixties, when Medina was director of the legal department of the National Institute of Agrarian Reform (INRA), Castro mentioned the prison conversation, recalling his own prescience: "Didn't I tell you they would kick you out!"

At the time of Medina's visit, Castro was deeply immersed in reconstructing his self-defense, which was finally published in October of that year. *La historia me absolverá* appeared in a mimeographed edition in Cuba and was printed in New York almost simultaneously.

The weekly *Bohemia* also focused attention on the Moncada group by promoting the amnesty campaign, launched early in 1955 by the prisoners' mothers and expanded into the Relatives' Amnesty Committee for Political Prisoners, with hundreds of members all over the island. As pressure for amnesty mounted, the regime tried to bargain with Castro for a conditional release. Predictably, he refused and instead drew up a statement signed by all the Moncada prisoners, which appeared in the March 25, 1955, issue of *Bohemia*. "Our personal freedom is an inalienable right as citizens of a nation that recognizes no master," read the statement. "We can be deprived of these and all other rights by force, but no one can ever make us agree to regain them by unworthy compromise. We won't give up one iota of our honor in return for our freedom."

On Friday, May 6, in deference to Mother's Day, Batista signed an unconditional amnesty law. On May 15, 1955, the *Moncadistas* walked out of prison into the welcoming arms of friends and relatives. At the Isle of Pines Hotel in Nueva Gerona, Castro gave a press conference before boarding the *Pinero* ferry for an all-night meeting with the men he hadn't seen in fourteen months. Crossing the shallow waters that separate the Isle of Pines from the main island, the group founded what would be known from then on as the Twenty-Sixth of July Movement.

With the rebels' release, Batista could turn his attention to the "orphan," as Medina had named the Isle of Pines. Recognizing "the situation of economic prostration" existing there, Batista declared the entire Isle and its offshore keys a free port—*zona franca especial*—exempt from taxes on production or merchandise, gross sales or purchases abroad, profits, surplus capital, dividends, income, revenue stamps, or anything else related to export and import.

Stimulated by the government Bank for Economic and Social Development (BANDES, pronounced "band-aids"), in conjunction with U.S. private capital, big chunks of territory were earmarked for the development of tourism, cattle ranching, industry, and urbanization.

The Gulf Caribbean Tourist Circuit, fronting for the New York mafia, planned to add several luxury hotels to those it already operated on the main island. The Colony Hotel, with its marble lobby and elite abortion clinic, was the only one actually built on the Isle, finished just in time for the rebels to take it over in 1959.

Drinking mineral water at Cotorro (Parrot) Springs in Santa Fé

Arthur V. Davis, president of the Aluminum Corporation of America, was a major investor in tourism industries and lodgings on the Isle. He acquired Bibijagua, the black-sand beach, and almost the entire southern part of the Isle. Davis also held 51 percent of the stock of Aerovias Q, which began transporting passengers and cargo to and from the new Nueva Gerona international airport as soon as it was opened in 1958. Aerovias Q connected with other points in Cuba and the southern United States.

For more than five decades, W. J. Mills monopolized maritime shipping with the Isle of Pines Steamship Company, which the family sold in 1956 to Cuban capitalists associated with Batista. In Santa Fé, a twenty-two-room motel with spring-fed pool and gym added modernity and comfort to the Santa Rita Springs Hotel of the twenties. The resort complex was renamed the Santa Fé Hotel, advertised as a "bargain paradise" for American tourists, especially retirees with a small income.

Cuban investors predominated in the purchase of smaller parcels of land sold at government auction for speculative urbanization. Many were farms abandoned over preceding decades by American settlers. The major latifundist in the north was an island cattle rancher named Gregorio Hernández (Goyo), who was also the financial force behind the expanding Banco de Fomento Comercial. The man was so powerful, according to his neighbors, that he controlled even the whims of nature. "When it rains on the Isle of Pines," people said bitterly, "it only rains on Goyo's land."

The Isle's infrastructure was also improved with new roads, water and sewage installations, and a bridge across Las Casas River. Arenas for bullfights and dog races were staked out with the approval of the National Sports Commission. Imports to the tax-free island soared as it became the gateway for merchandise—including drugs—destined for Havana. Local residents shared in the new prosperity as jobs and wages increased and low prices prevailed. Everybody was happy with the *zona franca*.

Andrés Fernández recalled: "The whole Isle was a free port and that meant no taxes on any product. I bought a new Chevrolet, tax-free. And, can you imagine French champagne and perfume without taxes? The idea was to protect the Isle, help the economy here. But they smuggled most of the goods into Havana, and that caused lots of trouble over there. It was a big problem. So, in 1959, the new government decided to end it. Fidel had a different idea of how to deal with things."

Mosako Harada faced a challenge: "I had to buy land from the big guys, because they were grabbing it all to build an aluminum factory, a refinery, hotels, and all kinds of companies. So, instead of selling, we bought from them and began to expand our farms, and that's how we saved the Japanese colony here."

Harry Koenig also staked out new claims: "After I got married, I bought some land out in Santa Barbara, and I had a truck. Sometimes I'd do a little trucking, or some mechanical work—did a little of everything. Around 1952 I opened a garage here in Gerona. I repaired cars and trucks and outboard motors, and I did body work. It wasn't the only garage. Cubans had garages, too. But when the Americans started coming back during the *zona franca,* I had a lot of work. See, retired people would come to the Isle, and they'd always come to me because I could talk English to them, you know."

Edith Sundstrom

Albert sold the hardware store to a Cuban and bought a dry dock. He built a warehouse, but that went down in the big storm of 1944. We lost that. We had the dry dock until Fidel took it away from us. Albert was always doing things to make more money. He represented several businesses on the Isle. He was agent for Texas Oil; he had a roofing paper business and some other small interests. Albert had to travel for his business every once in a while. Sometimes he would go alone, and sometimes I would go, too.

Then I used to go shopping in Havana with Mother once or twice a year, and she and Dad went to Miami a couple of times. But the four of us had never taken a family trip together. So, for their fiftieth wedding anniversary in 1953, Albert decided the four of us should tour Cuba. His idea was to start in Havana and go all the way to Santiago de Cuba, and that's just what we did. Albert contacted a friend who had a taxi service in Havana, and he took us everywhere we wanted to go, in a leisurely way with no fast driving. We stopped for a few days in Camagüey to visit Albert's nephew and his Cuban wife, continued to Santiago and spent some time there, then drove back. The driver was a wonderful person and became like one of the family. We all enjoyed every minute of the trip. Oh, I have very pleasant memories of the fifties. I don't recall any trouble under Batista.

Peggy Rice

After the war, Derek and Harry came back to the Isle, but only briefly. Derek returned to England, where he married and raised a family. Harry went back to Canada to have treatment for a war-related illness that turned out to be epilepsy, and married there. As soon as he could get the money together, he outfitted a boat and sailed down to visit the Isle with his wife.

My husband and I separated, and Maurice moved in with another woman. My friend Inez Fasser retired from nursing and bought a big place she converted into a guest house called Shangri-La, that she wanted me to manage with her. So I moved into Shangri-La with Joan and rented our house.

I did all the cleaning, washing, and cooking—we often had eight guests, and many times they would invite friends for dinner. It was a lot of work for me, but I enjoyed it. Inez took care of the business and did the planning and shopping for meals. I did the cooking and housekeeping. We were a good team, and Joan helped out, too, in her spare time.

Joan was growing up and becoming quite independent. Most weekends she spent swimming and horseback riding with her best friend, Aldah Wilkins, whose parents rented rooms in their vegetarian villa. The Wilkinses treated Joan like another daughter, and she loved being there, though she was always starving when she came home. I didn't realize the danger of eating raw vegetables until Joan was discovered to have parasites that finally developed into amoebas, a rather serious tropical disease.

We were very busy at Shangri-La. Our guests would recommend it to their friends, so we were always full. One day a new client took Inez aside and offered to purchase Shangri-La for a price she couldn't refuse. She decided to sell and use the profits to build a smaller guest house that we two could manage with less work, because she had been feeling tired. I told her to forget about a guest house altogether and to have a good, thorough checkup. Inez, of course, went right ahead with her plans.

Prior to Inez building her house, I went to England. I had saved some money and had an option on our house for $500. A fellow wanted to buy it but changed his mind, so of course he lost the option. I wanted to see dear old England and my family once more. The Wilkinses insisted that Joan stay with them. So I left on the SS Reina del Mar out of Havana in mid-May 1956. . . . We arrived in Plymouth at the end of May—the voyage took two weeks—and I traveled by train to London's Victoria Station, where my son and his wife met me with my first grandchild. They gave me a very nice welcome. My son's wife was expecting her second child when I stayed with them, and baby Paul was born during my visit.

Most of my time I spent with my three brothers at their respective homes. They were all overjoyed to see me for the first time since I left England in 1922. I came back from England at the end of September, during the hurricane season. We ran into the tail end of a storm, and it was terribly rough, impossible to get out of one's bunk for two days. I was happy to get back home.

A few months after my return, Joan turned eighteen. She had grown into a beautiful girl: blond hair and deep blue eyes, a lovely figure. She fell in love with a boy I didn't approve of because he was a mulatto. Most Cubans have a little colored blood. I had lived among colored people for a long time, and I liked them. And this was a very nice family. The boy's father was a doctor and director of the local hospital. But for my daughter to marry a colored person was a different matter. I believe they should marry their own kind; then the children don't suffer, one with white skin and one with dark skin. The poor little dark-skinned one wishes it were white, especially if it's a girl.

Much as I tried to dissuade Joan, Armando courted her very gallantly. His father had a big car, and he drove it. He always had money. Nothing a girl admires more when she is young. Joan was a very determined person, and nothing we could do or say would make her change her mind. They were married when she was eighteen. Harry came down from Canada to be best man at their wedding.

Through Armando's father, the newlyweds got their own small apartment at the hospital. They moved in with a nice bedroom suite they had managed to buy between them. Joan was working as a secretary to save money for the rest of the furnishings, and Armando did some odd jobs while looking into the possibility of studying medicine. They stayed married for five years, and the relationship went from bad to worse. They had decided to divorce, when Joan found out she was pregnant, so they thought they'd try once more. Joan hoped that, after the baby came, Armando would be more responsible. But nothing changed, and the divorce was granted.

Armando Valdés

*Armando de Jesús Valdés Rivas was my father, and I, the oldest
of his three sons, was named for him. He came to the Isle during
the Machado period, when it wasn't easy for a black doctor to secure a medical post. At first he was the only doctor in the small
hospital in Nueva Gerona, and my mother was the only nurse.
The patients paid for hospitalization, and any new equipment or
services came from contributions. When the revolution took over
all the hospitals in 1959, that one had thirty-two beds, and I
think there were three doctors on the medical staff. My father
was asked to remain as director because everyone on the island
knew and respected him. He wasn't a political person. He was a
man of science, but beyond his profession, he was very humanitarian. People trusted him.*

*The Twenty-Sixth of July Movement had a branch here in the
fifties, and I joined it when I was sixteen. We worked as an underground detachment, infiltrating members into the army,
navy, customs, and other key posts. I was assigned to the navy.
The Montané family was very involved in the movement because their son Jesús—Chucho, as we called him—had been with
Fidel at Moncada and then in prison here. The family was always very united, very generous. I consider Chucho a brother
because we're more or less contemporaries, and my father was
the Montané family doctor. Joan's brother Harry and Chucho
went to the American school together. They were buddies.*

*In those days, we all knew each other. The population was
small; people were friendly and respectful of each other. There
were lots of foreigners; a big migration of caimaneros made
them the largest group. Then there were the tourists, who came
for fishing, horseback riding, and the medicinal springs.*

*The south coast was another world. My brother Pepe and I
were the first to drive a jeep from Gerona to the south. Joan and*

her friend Aldah went with us. We had to cut our way through; there wasn't any road. People communicated by horse or by boat from Siguanea Bay, where the Colony Hotel now stands. The entire population on the south coast when we were there consisted of fifteen houses and a country store. I don't think it's much more now. Ah, but it certainly is beautiful.

Joan and I were married in 1957, when she had just turned eighteen and I was only nineteen. Margarita came along a few years later, and Joan gave birth at home. My father delivered the baby, and I received her. Her grandmother heated the water. At that time, nobody went to the hospital to give birth unless they had to.

Peggy Rice

Harry had just been divorced when Joan and Armando married. After their wedding, he decided to find a job on the Isle instead of returning to the cold of Canada. He got a job with a fellow here who had a tourist camp for fishing, hunting, etc. Harry was captain of one of the boats.

In the winter of 1958, he was doing what he liked best, taking people out cruising or fishing. Benny Goodman and his wife were among the tourists who came to the Isle to do a little fishing that season, and Harry was their captain and guide. While they were out at sea, Harry had an epileptic attack and fell into the water. Goodman quickly grabbed him and pulled him back into the boat. Harry was grateful to the famous orchestra leader for saving his life, but the accident also made him realize that sea work was too dangerous for him. He would rest up and return to Canada.

3 Changing the Face of the Isle

Every radio station carried news of the Rebel Army victory and dictator Batista's hurried departure from Cuba in the early morning hours of January 1, 1959. At the Model Prison on the Isle of Pines, some 600 political prisoners had declared circular 4 "free territory of Cuba," admitting prison guards only for a head count. The Twenty-Sixth of July Movement, swelled by the capture of expeditionaries from the *Granma* landing, numbered about 500 men, organized under the leadership of Armando Hart.[1] Another 30 members of student and political groups and 70 military opponents of Batista completed the rebel roll call. At Hart's request, one of the imprisoned army officers, José Ramón Fernández,[2] had been training a battalion of Twenty-Sixth of July prisoners in military operations.

While prison officials negotiated their inevitable replacement by the rebel inmates, Hart proposed to Fernández that he act as military commander of the Isle, subordinate to the Twenty-Sixth of July Movement, and Fernández accepted. On the fortieth anniversary of that fateful takeover, Fernández recalled how it was organized:

What were Hart, the Twenty-Sixth of July Movement, and I thinking, very rationally? To secure the Isle. Hopefully, nothing would happen to block the revolution from taking power, but if something did happen, we controlled an island with a seaport and an airport that were inaccessible to the Batista forces. We could block any landing. We had a bastion, with a radio and everything else we needed. We had a self-sufficient island.

I went to the barracks and introduced myself as the new military chief of the Isle. There were some eighty or ninety soldiers, eighty policemen, and some guards. I ordered them to put the weapons in the armory. Then I took a vehicle and went to circular 4, because my force was there, in the battalion I had trained and in the military prisoners. The gate was opened, and the comrades began leaving, but it seems that someone also opened the gate to circular 3, where the most noted criminals were held, and those common prisoners fled en masse. The machine gun outside our circular began firing; fortunately no one was hurt. I had to halt the fire by opening the cover because the gunners—probably more nervous than anything else—ignored the cease fire order.

At the barracks, I armed all the political prisoners, assigned them their posts, and then we undertook to capture the common prisoners who had escaped. After that we detained other delinquents, such as former prison director Capote, who lived nearby. He was tried and shot to death, not for anything he had done to us, but for previous crimes against common prisoners.

The Isle of Pines was secured by triumphant rebels who marched in combat detachments to occupy the Rural Guard, navy, customs, and other key posts without firing a shot.[3]

PROJECTING DREAMS

After a helicopter inspection of the Isle of Pines, Castro addressed a mass meeting in Nueva Gerona on June 7, 1959, to outline priorities for development and change.[4]

The first priority was tourism, which would include the construction of new hotels and recreation facilities for residents and visitors, direct flights from Florida to encourage Americans to come, and a network of roads connecting all parts of the island. The luxurious Colony Hotel, already nationalized, was designated for international tourism; more modest hotels would be built for national tourism.

Agriculture was the second priority, with special emphasis on pasture lands for the cattle that would supply the island with meat and milk; grapefruit would be grown in abundance, for domestic consumption and export; truck farming would supply plenty of fresh fruits and vegetables; and a great reforestation program was planned. A network of reservoirs and irrigation systems would ensure a stable water supply and provide new recreational areas.

Industry related to the island's resources, production, and needs was the third priority. Kaolin for ceramics and construction materials such as tiles, bricks, marble, and cement were vital to development.

Educational, medical, and social services would be expanded, communications improved, and the Model Prison phased out as a penitentiary.

These were the dreams, and Castro discussed "creating the conditions" to make them come true. For a start, it would be necessary to nullify the popular but divisive tax-free zone that gave the Isle and its residents certain acquisitive preferences over other areas. Although some of his advisers had suggested issuing a proclamation or edict to that effect, Castro decided to bring the matter to the vote of the masses, then and there, never doubting the outcome after they had heard his arguments. When he called for raised hands to eliminate the *zona franca,* the vote was as close to unanimous as the camera could record. Even people like Andrés Fernández, who cherished his tax-free Chevrolet, thought it only just to eliminate such geographic favoritism.

Farmers, agronomists, engineers, builders, students, and workers laid out the projects for the Isle, dividing the latifundia into eight state farms that covered almost as much territory as the original seven *haciendas* of the eighteenth century. Location and soil evaluation determined where new citrus groves would be added to those still yielding fruit from the early years of the twentieth century. Fields of onions, cucumbers, tomatoes, and melons were bordered by acres of black beans and sorghum. The first national cattle ranch for breeding the F1—a cross between native Cebú and Holstein—was started in 1960, with more than 2,000 acres of pasture for grazing. Other farms were devoted to chickens, pigs, goats, and sheep.

Small private farms were restricted in size, and the individual who owned or worked each parcel was incorporated into the newly created National Association of Small Farmers (ANAP). The Japanese farmers, always the most productive on the Isle, continued to operate in family cooperatives. Other small properties and businesses were also restricted or liquidated.

Harry Koenig

Well, after the government changed, they took my garage away. First they said it was mine because, according to the law, I had been paying rent for more than fifteen years and that made me the owner of the property I had been renting. So I went and got the ownership papers. Then, a little later, they came back and said it was illegal to have a private business, and they liquidated me. They didn't compensate me. Al contrario, *they went over all the tax receipts and told me the taxes weren't paid up, that I owed them the difference for five years back. I had to pay $4,000. They did that to a lot of people. A friend of mine who had a trucking business was told he owed $10,000 in back taxes on his property.*

You couldn't own any business, and the garage was in my name. Luckily, my brother was able to keep the boat, and I kept the pickup. I had it until I fell and broke my hip, and then I couldn't use it, so I sold it.

If you had too much land, they took part of that away, too; but I lost my property because I had come into town to live, and they made a dam out there, and the property went below water. So now I have this house and the land it's on—I finally got the property rights. It's a very small plot, but in my backyard, which is about as big as this room, I used to plant lettuce and things when I could get around. And I have a pension of eighty pesos a month.

Mosako Harada

After the revolution, the government claimed some of the land. We had a cooperative of sixteen caballerías *[one* caballería *equals thirty-three acres], but some of it was poor land with lots of rocks and weeds. I had to turn over some of the cattle to the government, too. Then, with the second agrarian reform, you couldn't keep more than five* caballerías. *That meant two-thirds for the government and a third for us. We had to dissolve the coop to save the land. That way, each farmer kept the permitted acreage. Then we could reform the coop. The government didn't touch us because everything was in order here. Everyone spoke well of me. They said I was open and honest and my prices were fair. Everything was in good shape and running smoothly. They liked that, and that's the way it's always been.*

Kesano Harada

For me there wasn't much change. I've never had anything to do with politics—or with the land, for that matter, except to work on it. So I kept on doing what I had always done, which was farming. I had help from the older children, who were all grown by that time. The younger ones helped, too, but when they had a chance to study, they went to school so they could learn about other things besides farming.

Edith Sundstrom

We had to give up one car when the revolution came, but they never searched our home like they did Peggy's. They took our business, but Albert was paid for the dry dock. Many people— Cubans, even—had their businesses taken away from them, and they weren't paid anything. Albert was fortunate. They paid us $10,000. Albert used to say it was worth two or three times that much, but anyhow we got something. We lived on that and what we had in the bank. We never were rich people, and we always had a good way of life.

Peggy Rice

With the profits from the sale of her Shangri-La Motel, Inez built this seven-room house, with two bathrooms and porches, on an acre of land planted with fruit trees; and there's a little bungalow out back. Inez wanted a place big enough to take in one or two boarders. We could easily handle that together, she said, and make some money, too. Then, in 1958, shortly after we moved in, Inez became very ill with cancer. She went to Havana for an operation, and her health seemed to improve for a while. But she had a series of strokes and died here in the summer of 1959.

Inez had willed all her property to me, and, of course, I contin-
ued to live here, but I had quite a time trying to prove my own-
ership to officials of the new government. They arrived at the
door and said they had come to take the house. They were al-
ready moving the chairs out when I said, "But you can't do this.
The house belongs to me." I got them to wait until I could see the
British consul, and we managed to get it all straightened out. I
have lived here since then without being molested in any way.

I remember Harry was still here in 1959 but had decided to re-
turn to Canada to work there. He left the island with five dollars.
That is all our new communist government would allow him to
take. He arrived in the States and slept for one week in the bus
station until, with some help from a friend, he managed to get
back to Canada.

There were great changes on the Isle, of course. We were ra-
tioned, and food was scarce, but we were not hungry. Fidel has
done a lot in construction: housing and schools, both badly
needed; good transportation all over the Isle; plenty of service to
Havana by plane, in a fast hydrofoil launch called the Kometa
and by passenger/cargo ferry; outdoor movies; an ice cream par-
lor. . . .

I met Fidel when he first visited the Isle—he was in prison
here before he was famous, but we didn't know anything about
him then. I met him when he came in 1959. I think he's an aw-
fully nice chap.

The Isle's resident workforce was inadequate for the vast development plans. Initially, waves of students and workers came from all
parts of the country for a forty-five-day stint in agriculture. They
were housed in hastily built barracks, and most of what they consumed had to be imported from the main island. Sometimes there was
no drinking water in the field, and often they walked to and from
work. They were willing, but inexperienced, farmers. Many would

later confess that those forty-five days seemed like eternity. Units of the Rebel Army added their manpower in reforestation, eating and sleeping in the tents that identified their temporary military camps. The soldiers planted 700,000 eucalyptus seedlings before they were called to active duty to defend the island's coasts.

These initial advances were barely visible in the summer of 1960, when a group of visiting Americans enamored with the revolution flew over from Havana to see where its leader and his rebel friends had been imprisoned. From the small airport, we drove along narrow roads through the two small towns of Nueva Gerona and La Fé and on to the Model Prison, enormous in comparison to any other structure on the Isle. The common prisoners had all been transferred to provincial detention centers near their homes for reclassification; but the tiers housed a new variety of political prisoners: men convicted of counterrevolutionary crimes against the government headed by Fidel Castro. In the hospital wing, we saw the leader's former isolation cell and the men's ward, sparsely furnished with rows of neatly made iron beds.

In April 1961 Cuban mercenaries financed and trained in the United States launched their doomed invasion at Playa Girón (Bay of Pigs), on the Zapata Peninsula, northeast of the Isle of Pines. Defending the Isle's coasts on April 17, the patrol boat *Baire* was strafed by enemy plane fire that killed two and wounded eleven crew members. When the new hospital was constructed on the Isle a few years later, it was named *Heroes del Baire* in honor of those victims.

The Bay of Pigs attack provoked a dramatic turn in Cuban history, when Castro declared that the Cuban revolution would henceforth be socialist. Instead of tourist flights from Florida, there would be oil from the Soviet Union, and weapons, too. In 1962, by mutual agreement between Cuba and the USSR, the Soviets installed nuclear missiles along the north coast of the main island. Khrushchev withdrew the missiles during a confrontation with President Kennedy, and nuclear warfare was averted. Cuban territory remained intact, but the country was ostracized and isolated from the rest of the Americas, placed under a U.S. commercial and travel embargo. For thirty years, until socialism collapsed in eastern Europe, Cuba looked to the Soviet Union for aid, trade, and technology.

On the Isle of Pines, as elsewhere in Cuba, development was still in the project stage in 1962, so it was easy enough to put international tourism on the back burner and concentrate on agriculture. With the emphasis on state farms and cooperatives, the small private farmers—mostly Caymanians—were marginalized, and many left in 1965 on a boat lift that departed from the bay of Camarioca, in Matanzas Province. Then, in June 1966, Hurricane Alma struck the Isle, destroying more than 2,000 acres of fruits, vegetables, and nursery plants; hundreds of heads of cattle; and thousands of chickens.

As a rallying force, though, Alma was fortuitous. A call for help went out, and 1,500 Communist Youth arrived that same month to help pick up the pieces. Youngsters from all over Cuba continued to respond through their schools and local organizations, as "Followers of Camilo and Che," the two exemplary revolutionaries.

Magaly Reyes, a bright-eyed, energetic twenty-year-old, came in one of the first groups from Havana, "para trabajar en lo que fuera"—to work wherever needed. "There was nothing here," she recalled thirty years later, "three small towns with a cluster of houses, no sewage, no highways. We lived in tents at first, later in rustic barracks, and worked in the surrounding fields digging holes and planting pasture." Magaly fell in love with the Isle and with a man who shared her commitment "to make the future" there. A year later, their future included an infant daughter.

Twenty-four-year-old Juan Colina was married and the father of two little girls, but he left his family in Havana to join the first construction contingent that came to the Isle early in 1967. The family arrived the following year—in time to inaugurate the Coppelia ice cream parlor Juan had helped build. He, his wife, their three daughters, and a couple of grandchildren were living in Gerona at the end of the century.

Magaly Reyes and Juan Colina were a minority among the 4,500 young people who came to work on the Isle that first year after the hurricane. Both were from Havana, were high school graduates, and were a few years older than the majority of arrivals from the provincial cities of eastern Cuba with whom they worked.

The year 1967 saw endless movement on the Isle. Trucks loaded with people and animals, tools and equipment, plants and fertilizers, food and supplies moved back and forth across new roads to construction works and recently planted fields. Radio Caribe began broadcasting locally, and *Victoria*'s first weekly editions appeared with exhortatory headlines, upbeat photos of workers, and long economic reports printed in small type (later, as a daily, the paper added crossword puzzles, caricatures, and short features). At every meeting of cadres, the discussion turned to Che Guevara's vision of creating a communist model while building socialism.

In August of that year, Castro came to inaugurate the island's first reservoir, Viet Nam Heroico, which flooded over a few farms to provide irrigation for some 96,000 additional acres of land. The project, he said, was the first attempt to protect the island's crops from both excessive and insufficient rainfall; he congratulated the young people who had worked tirelessly to finish it in record time. When the youngsters clamored to rename the island Isle of Youth, Castro gave them a list of goals they had to achieve before that could happen.

"Here we propose not only to revolutionize nature, but also to revolutionize minds, to revolutionize society," he told them. "Why not also aspire to make this the first communist region in Cuba?" (*Granma*, 8-8-68).

The response was a roar of approval. Why not, indeed! In that euphoric climate, communism lay at the end of the next furrow. In striving to attain it, young workers would collectively become the new man, geared to production, not possession, free of greed and the consumer mentality. Passionately, they discussed the possibility of eliminating money, which they considered the root of all evil.

Indeed, money had little meaning in the youth labor camps, where lodgings, food, work, clothes, medical care, education, and even mobile beauty parlors were provided by the government. By year's end, wages were generally set between sixty-five and eighty-five pesos a month, with no paid overtime. This forced out the "peso hunters" who had been earning high wages and overtime as unskilled workers in the construction brigades. It also set general parameters for the future, so that those who had come for a temporary stay could then leave or make a new commitment for an indefinite stay.

Housing was scarce and inadequate in those early days, especially for families. A few barracks were partitioned to accommodate couples and their children until the construction brigades could provide better accommodations. The Colina family lived that way for nearly two years while Juan continued in construction and Isora worked in agriculture, after arranging day care for their youngsters.

Magaly always remembered carrying her baby to the field with the rest of the brigade workers "because I didn't want to be left behind." She would spread out a blanket in the shade of a tree and keep the child in sight while she worked. It was that bucolic setting, she claimed facetiously, that influenced her daughter to become an agronomist.

While some of the camps were integrated, most were all male or all female. The *brigadistas* were assigned to a dormitory, where each person had a cot and a bedside stand or crate for minimal toiletries and personal belongings. The camp regime was semi-military: wake-up music blared before 6 A.M., and, after a quick breakfast of coffee with milk and a piece of bread, the campers were trucked off to work from 7 A.M. to noon, with *merienda* (the quintessential snack) around 9:30. They returned to camp, showered, ate, and rested from noon to 2 P.M., then worked again until 5 or 5:30, with a pause for afternoon *meri-*

enda. Back at camp, they played games, bathed, and lined up for dinner—usually rice and beans, beef or chicken in a light gravy, stewed fruit, and bread served into the depressions of a tin tray and eaten with a spoon at trestle tables. Afterwards there were classes, discussion groups, and recreation until lights out at 10.

Once a week, the campers were given a pass to go into town, where they could see a movie and eat ice cream. The regime was frequently off schedule because of long lines for meals, endless waits for transportation, and an excess of revolutionary lecturing. Everything was massive and noisy, collectively organized for unruly adolescents.

Infractions of camp regulations—such as fighting, stealing, or staying out all night—were severely punished and could lead to expulsion from the camp and the island, as determined by the camp leadership.

One camp director reported to her platoon the expulsion of two *compañeras* found in a truck at two o'clock in the morning with two *compañeros* "in a way that was not correct."[5] The *compañeros* were from a nearby camp and had also been expelled. Another girl had stayed in town all night and still hadn't returned to camp. Punishment had already been meted out, but the director wanted everyone else to understand that "we cannot make this island the first site of communism in Cuba with such people." Then she invited them to comment on the matter.

When one of the girls said she thought it would be "all right at the movies perhaps—but not in a truck," the director looked startled and insisted that "this wasn't a matter of a boy with his arms around a girl."

A few titters moved the director to address the lofty goal of making their camp "the most prestigious and best on the island for the upcoming anniversary of the founding of the Communist Youth League. We must all work to achieve this; we must work very hard," she said earnestly. "Now, it's time to bathe."

There was plenty of criticism of the youngsters from other sources, too. They were careless, uninterested, and slow, according to experienced farmers who supervised their work. "But," said one, "when *merienda* comes, watch them move."[6] If *merienda* didn't come, or came very late, a sitdown was the rule; and when everything was on schedule, a noisy fight might break out over cheating to get the "extra" *merienda* that really belonged to someone else.

Shortly before her death in 1970 at age ninety-two, Evangelina Cossio, that rebellious adolescent of 1896, commented caustically on Cuban youth: "I don't like the queues and I don't like the behavior of young people. A great deal must be done to educate these rowdy youngsters; they don't respect their elders and they think everything falls from the sky" (*Bohemia*, 1967).

The "rowdy youngsters" took everything in stride. More and more arrived, production goals and collective improvement were set at ever higher levels, and new projects were constantly incorporated into the overall development plan. At an evaluation ("criticism and self-criticism") assembly held in late October 1967, representatives of all the organizations on the Isle agreed that workers' consciousness was at an all-time high but that the instability of the workforce was itself problematic. In less than a decade, the population had tripled from 10,000 to 30,000. Most of the immigration was from the five easternmost provinces of Santiago de Cuba, Guantánamo, Granma, Holguín, and Las Tunas, followed by Ciudad de la Habana.[7] Ninety-nine percent of the workforce came from somewhere else, including the enormous floating population of professionals, students, and skilled and unskilled workers.

The small farmers who had been working their land before 1959 made up the other 1 percent of the workforce as members of ANAP, through which they received seeds, fertilizers, and a local market. In 1969 there were around 260 who owned an average of two *caballerías* (sixty-six acres) each.[8]

Augustus Forrest, then age sixty-six, was one, a blue-eyed, gray-haired mulatto with a weathered face and strong body who spoke English slowly and well. Ten years later, while Gus and his partner

Rulle Ebanks were loading melons in the field, the truck tipped over and trapped Gus beneath it. He died a few days later.

CRIME AND JUSTICE

The bloody bodies of Ilse Sperlin Zeidler, age fifty-six, a refugee from Hitler's Austria who had become a Cuban citizen, and William Jones Gaines, sixty-four, a U.S. citizen from South Carolina and retired FBI agent, were discovered by their part-time Cayman housekeeper when she let herself in through the back door of the isolated house on Monday morning, November 13, 1967.[9]

The housekeeper ran out to the road and flagged down a police jeep to report the crime. Within a short time, forensics experts were on the scene, and departures from the Isle were under surveillance.

Gaines had been killed by machete blows. His head and face were smashed, and every bone in his shoulders and hands broken. The gore was partially covered with a sheet, but the bloody machete lay exposed beside the body. Zeidler's face was bruised, and her thighs were black and blue. She had been strangled to death with an electric cord. A sharp knife lay on the night table next to the bed.

Every drawer and closet in the house was open, pointing to robbery as the motive for the crime. Documents found in the bedroom verified the testimony of friends that William and Ilse were planning to leave the island for the United States via Mexico. They would certainly have had a considerable amount of cash and other valuables in the house to take with them.

News of the murders spread by word of mouth, consuming residents with fear. Brutal killers on the loose. How many? Where would they strike next? Especially terrifying to the older immigrants was the fact that the victims were also foreign, English-speaking, and longtime island residents. At once, they began barring windows and doors.

In her own isolated house several kilometers from where the murders had been committed, Peggy Rice shook her head in disbelief. Nothing like it had ever happened in all her years on the Isle. Peggy had known Ilse for twenty years, William for fifteen—since they had made their separate ways to the Isle with other partners. She had accepted their recent union of convenience, their decision to leave the Isle now that everything had changed. Peggy was their friend without being close to them, for she never felt really comfortable with Ilse's Sephardic heritage of displacement and intensity, much less William's smug superiority. Nevertheless, they belonged to what was called "the American community," which included all white, middle-class English-speaking residents. It was a small but visible community, and everybody else on the island treated its members with tolerance and respect.

To Peggy, it was unthinkable that the murderers were islanders. The crime was too brutal. Only barbarians could have done such a thing. Just imagine chopping up two people and then calmly robbing them! Peggy was glad she had nothing of value in her house, though that wouldn't stop a maniac. She was very much relieved that Joan and her boyfriend were moving in because she would have been quite frightened to continue living alone with the baby. She didn't mind at all that Joan's *novio* was bringing his gun.

Tension mounted as the investigation zeroed in on two workers in the construction camp nearest the scene of the crime. Blood tests, material evidence, work attitudes, personal history, criminal records, interviews—all the factors that could exonerate the innocent or convict the guilty were examined and introduced at the public trial held on December 1 in the main square of Nueva Gerona. The square was filled, and a few people perched in trees as the presiding judge opened trial 1912-67 of the Revolutionary Tribunal of the District of Havana.

Marcelino Leyva Zamora, twenty-seven, and Rolando González Vines, twenty-one, both of Oriente Province, were charged with double murder and robbery. Their own testimony confirmed all the forensic evidence against them, which included blood stains and fingerprints on the weapons used. Marcelino (black), from Bayamo, emerged as the instigator of the crime, and Rolando, or Jabao (a sandy-haired mulatto), from Palma Soriano, as a willing accomplice. Neither showed any remorse for bludgeoning William to death, nor for raping and choking Ilse. "The dead don't talk," they had agreed, as they ransacked the house and departed with a suitcase of loot. They hid the suitcase and divided the money (Marcelino took 2,000 pesos and gave Jabao 1,000); then they bathed, ate, and went to bed.

In the construction brigade where they earned close to 200 pesos a month, both were known as "conflictive," ill-tempered, foul-mouthed, brutish. Marcelino was an escaped convict who had served less than half of a fourteen-year sentence for stabbing his stepmother to death. From Oriente, he made his way to Havana and then to the Isle of Pines, where he committed his last brutal murder.

Jabao had walked out on his first and second wives and had never sent either of them anything from his earnings to support the three children he had fathered. His family was as dead to him as those two foreigners, but this time he couldn't walk away.

After weighing all the evidence, the court returned a unanimous verdict of guilty on all counts for both defendants. The perpetrators of the most horrendous crime ever committed on the Isle were shot to death by a firing squad early the next morning.

In retrospect, the event that had riveted the island's attention for eighteen days in 1967 came to be regarded as an ugly aberration in a decade of promise. Yet a shadow of fear, tinged with prejudice against young black men from the eastern provinces, continued to haunt the island.

During the sixties, more than a few prisoners convicted of crimes against the revolution were paroled from the Model Prison as graduates of the "Three Steps to Freedom" reeducation program consisting of lectures, studies, and work.

Such was the case of a former bakery owner who had been imprisoned for sabotage. After serving three years of a ten-year sentence, one year of which he spent in reeducation, he was released and employed as a bakery supervisor on the Isle. Officially classified as rehabilitated, he was accepted by his coworkers with a live-and-let-live attitude, no questions asked. He was working at a productive job and that was enough.[10]

During that period, a handful of counterrevolutionary prisoners in rehabilitation at the Model Prison formed a theater group and dramatized their experiences as *La Libertad a tres pasos*, which they performed for various prison audiences and at the national assembly of the Women's Federation held in the Colony Hotel in 1965.[11] Prime Minister Fidel Castro attended that performance by young men who had been his sworn enemies only a few months earlier. Then the group went public with the hit, and, after a successful run of several months, the actors disbanded and were granted conditional freedom to live and work normally.

One of them continued performing with a Havana group for another year, until two members of the Communist Youth came to the theater one day and asked for volunteers to work on the Isle of Pines for two years. Perhaps pressured by his parole status, he raised his hand and soon found himself back on the Isle, assigned to the prison tile factory where he had worked in the reeducation program. It was no secret that he was a former prisoner, and some of his coworkers were impressed that he had the fortitude to volunteer for a job in the prison where he had once been confined. While he was fulfilling his work commitment, he married, became a father, and taught theater in his spare time. At the end of two years, he decided to stay on because, as he told his wife, "for the moment, I think I'm more useful in production than on the stage."[12]

In 1967 the Model Prison was deactivated and its cell bars removed. Prisons were decentralized in a provincial system where the same principles of work and reeducation were applied. In one tiered building of the former Model Prison, a technological institute for the study of soils, fertilizers, and cattle raising operated for a time, and other areas were used for offices, storage, and a museum gallery. In 1986 the Pioneer Headquarters was opened there, and youngsters from all over the Isle began participating in hobby clubs, sports, entertainment, and field trips. By 1997 more than 35,000 young students had passed through the institution, according to its director, Marcos Alexis Cadena (*Granma*, 15-8-97).

Meanwhile, the older model for the Model Prison, Stateville Prison in Joliet, Illinois, was still a penitentiary in 1997. Operating in a single round bloc "under horrible conditions," according to U.S. prison historian Merrill Dodge, the original 1,000 cells designed for single confinement were being used as double cells "with subsequent overcrowding and lack of recreation or rehabilitation or jobs."[13]

STUDY AND WORK

In 1961 the first elementary boarding school opened on the Isle of Pines in a rambling farmhouse formerly owned by an American couple who had raised hunting dogs. There, 167 first to sixth graders from Nueva Gerona and La Fé studied and helped produce the food they ate. Within two years, the farm-school was self-sufficient in eggs, chicken, pork, and vegetables, and the project was expanded to accommodate a total of 300 youngsters, who boarded during the week and went home on weekends.[14]

In a very short time, every neighborhood had its day elementary school (in existing or new buildings), and most were also used at night for adult literacy classes. In this early period of educational expansion, Havana supplied the Isle with teachers and methodology, and the construction brigades built the new facilities. The goal was a sixth-grade education for everyone. Double sessions were the rule in the primary schools until, by 1968, there were enough teachers and classrooms to switch to all-day schedules. That year, too, the first junior high and technical schools were established so that sixth-grade graduates no longer had to leave the Isle to continue their studies. Working mothers had day care for their toddlers, and some on-job training programs included basic reading, writing, and arithmetic for adults. Everyone, it seemed, went to school.

In the 1970s, mass education on the Isle reached the secondary level with the establishment of junior-and senior-high boarding schools in the countryside and the technical institutes and university branches that would eventually graduate the Isle's professional cadres.

Castro inaugurated the first Escuela Secondaria Basica en el Campo (ESBEC), or Junior High School in the Countryside, in 1971. All the students on the Isle eligible for junior high school—more than 200— were enrolled in the first year's course, and, since the school was built to accommodate 500 students, the remaining capacity was filled by sixth graders. The prefabricated installation, named 14 de junio (the birth date of Antonio Maceo and Ernesto Guevara), was set in 1,320 acres of citrus orchards—this was the equivalent of almost all the citrus under cultivation before the revolution—and the students tended the orchards. The school was staffed by forty teachers and fifty administrative, technical, and service workers.

Commenting on this auspicious beginning of secondary education, Castro said: "When we have some 30,000 students here in schools of this type, then this will truly be, with every right, the Isle of Youth."[15]

Six years later, the Isle had twenty-six junior high schools and three senior high schools for boarders, each with capacities and facilities equal to the first. Beginning that year of 1977, in response to agreements with party leaders, young Angolans and Mozambicans entered junior high schools set up for them with the same privileges (free tuition, board, and room plus a monthly stipend) and responsibilities (study and work) as their island contemporaries. Within a few years, there were enough students on the Isle to eliminate the need for mobilizations from other provinces for agricultural work.

Margarita Valdés Rice

I was born in 1961 in the little house out back, not in the hospital. My father's father was a doctor, a gynecologist, and he delivered me. My dad knows about medicine too, but he's not a doctor. He didn't finish the career. Well, my parents broke up when I was just a baby. My dad went to Havana. My mom stayed and remarried—they had a little house down there with lots of animals.

I lived here with Granny. I've always been "Shug" to Gran, and she took care of me all the time I was growing up. Most of the time we lived together alone. One night when just the two of us were here, somebody tried to rob the house, but Granny woke up and scared them off. This was around 1967 or 1968, when we had a lot of foreign people here from the rest of the country, even people who had been in prison.

My grandfather was robbed too, in his own place. He used to fix watches and jewelry, and they came and tied him to a chair and put a rag in his mouth and cleared his place out. Mommy went down to see him and she found him like that, so we moved him up here into the small house in back. He used to make me little airplanes, and he invented lots of things. He used to write poems, too. He was a very smart man. He knew a lot, and he drank a lot. Then he got sick, and Gran took care of him until he died.

When I started school, they had a session for the girls in the morning and one for the boys in the afternoon. It was a very poor school, and the teaching methods weren't the same as now.

It was the beginning. There were hardly any teachers or any schools before the revolution, so they both came little by little.

After I finished sixth grade, I went to the Tupac Amaru[16] Junior High School. That's where my daughter Jackie is now. When I went, it was the beginning of the boarding school program on the Isle. It was better then than it is now; there was more organization, the children used to help each other more, everything was in order and tidy. We worked outside half the day, picking grapefruit or chopping grass, and had classes the other half. My grades were so-so, but I wasn't really interested in school. I didn't like the outdoor work, and I didn't like being there all week. My mom wasn't well, and I preferred being at home.

We were living here together then, and Mommy was sick all the time with parasites. She was treated and was better for a while. And she kept on working, always. She was a secretary. She used to do clerical work. She would leave early and come back at six every afternoon. I always waited for her. She was very affectionate with me. She usually came home tired. But then she'd have a drink, smoke a cigarette, put on shorts, and go out with the mowing machine to cut the grass or clip the hedges. My mom had about five cats, several dogs, two parrots, a big pen of chickens. She liked lots of trees. She liked her garden—we used to plant all sorts of stuff for the kitchen. Outside of that, she didn't have any social life, going out with friends; she wasn't that kind of a person.

I had a boyfriend, and I wanted to marry him and start a family. I was only fourteen years old, so my mother had to give her permission. My father wasn't here. He was in Angola—he was in one of the first contingents that went to Angola. So I got married during that time when mommy was half sick and half well. Then she got very ill and, nearly on my birthday, when I was about to turn fifteen, she passed away.

It hurt to lose my mother just when I needed her most, when I

*was going into the world without knowing anything about it.
Gran used to advise me a lot, but to me it wasn't the same as my
mom, who was closer to my age and had always worked outside
the house, in an office where you meet people with different
ideas from your family.*

From Peggy Rice's diary

*Joan took very ill in March of 1976. A lump had formed at the
base of her stomach. She couldn't eat, had no appetite, took
much medicine to no avail. Finally, we persuaded her to go to
the hospital. An operation was necessary, which was fatal. She
had cancer. The end came on July 13, 1976. She was so young,
only 38.*

*Harry was wonderful. As soon as he received the wire that
Joan had passed on, he was down here to the island to be with
me and comfort me. It was his second trip in just a few months
and a big expense for him, but he was happy to come, very sad
at Joan's passing because he was truly fond of his sister.*

*So we continue to go on day by day in spite of our sorrow.
Margarita is now expecting a baby and we are busy planning for
the new life that is coming. I pray all will be well with Shug as
she is so young to have a child. She has to visit her doctor every
week and, once a month, has analyses of blood, urine, weight;
and she has a special diet. They take very good care of pregnant
mothers here at no cost. Such a change from the old days when
the hospital in Gerona had hardly any beds or equipment, very
little linen, very few doctors and very few women to clean the
wards.*

*In May of 1977, I had the misfortune to break my leg up high
and splinter my hip bone. They fixed me up with pieces of steel
and what looked like screws in the x-ray picture. Then I was
doomed to stay put for four months. I realize I am very lucky at
my age for my leg to have healed. I have had very bad luck with*

broken bones: one broken wrist, a broken ankle, right leg and
now left leg. I must have very brittle bones. From now on I shall
have to be very careful and watch every step.

ISLE OF YOUTH

In August 1978, while Cuba was hosting the Eleventh World Youth
Festival in Havana, the Isle of Pines officially became the Isla de la
Juventud, or Isle of Youth. Raúl Roa, Cuba's venerated "foreign minister of dignity," as he was called in the sixties, returned to the Isle,
where he had been a youthful political prisoner, to celebrate the occasion with Cuban, Angolan, Mozambican, and Ethiopian students and
residents of the Isle.

"Little by little the colossal commitment to convert the Isle of Pines
into the Isle of Youth spread among successive waves of young people
who came to work on it," Roa said. "But that meant moving here.
With transients, you could never transform society and nature. And
now, the face of the island has changed. Its resident population has
quadrupled, with young people in the lead" (*Juventud Rebelde*, 4-8-
78).

By the mid-eighties, forty-five junior and eight senior high schools
were functioning on the Isle. They were named Tupac Amaru, Copernico, Pablo de la Torriente Brau, Clara Zetkin—each one recalling
some historic figure or event. In fifteen years, these schools graduated
nearly 35,000 students. At other levels of education, the Isle had
twenty-six day-care centers; seventy-five elementary schools; thirteen night schools; a gamut of technical institutes for aspiring agronomists, athletes, and nurses; and a Teachers' Training College.

Education for the masses was not without its problems on the Isle,
and most were too generalized to be ignored for very long: few and
underqualified teachers; overcrowded classrooms; inflexible and un-
imaginative teaching methods; profiteering with school supplies and
facilities; petty theft by employees and students; lack of discipline,

especially in agricultural work; hygienic and sanitary inadequacies; deterioration and wanton destruction of installations and furniture; and what one educator called "absolute lack of control."

At one junior high, students celebrated the end of the 1980 school year by smashing windows, breaking furniture, and stealing supplies, for which they and their parents were tried and sentenced to rebuild the entire school at their own expense. Students from Havana who attended boarding schools on the Isle in the late seventies and early eighties were appalled by the terrible sanitary conditions and general chaos. Coming from the big city or a protective family, a young girl could be traumatized by the absolute isolation of her school. What would happen in case of a serious accident, a sudden illness, or attempted rape by some evil intruder (this last was a frequently repeated, if unsubstantiated, concern in the girls' dorms)?

When problems in the schools became too blatant or widespread, an investigation would follow. Early in 1982, for instance, educational authorities launched Operation Vulture to end pilfering and admin-

Fishing boats on Las Casas River in Gerona

istrative negligence in some junior highs in Havana and on the Isle of Youth, and they reported on the operation in the party newspaper *Granma*.[17]

Edith Sundstrom, Miami, 1991

Our quiet little island had totally changed. Suddenly there were all these big, ugly buildings and people, people everywhere. We got schools, roads, a great big hospital, a packinghouse, and all kinds of things we never had before. But something of the beauty was taken away.

At the same time, there were lots of things we couldn't get, like lobster and shrimp (the only fish we got was the worst). Plenty of rice, but I never liked rice. And it wasn't like the old days when you could go shopping and find what you wanted some-where, at some price. There wasn't any place you could spend U.S. dollars. You had to exchange them for Cuban pesos at the rate of two dollars for every peso.

Though there were lots of changes we didn't quite understand, we weren't molested in any way. We still had our little casita with its beautiful garden. That was our home, and mother's too, after dad died. We never considered going back to the States. Albert was Cuban, and we both loved the island. We had nothing in the States—no close relatives, no property, no money.

Then, in 1978, I lost my family. My mother and my husband both died that year. It was quite a blow, and I sort of went to pieces for a bit. Mother was ninety-five and had lived a full life. I grieved for her, but I could accept her death. Losing Albert, though, was like losing part of myself. We had a wonderful life, a wonderful home. He was a wonderful husband. It seemed that everybody in town came by to console me. Everyone knew Albert and loved him. I don't think Albert ever had an enemy in Nueva Gerona.

One of the callers was a young man named Alexis Rosa, who taught high-school English. Peggy and I had met him in town one day when we went to see a Marilyn Monroe movie. We talked a while then, and he came by the house once or twice after that to practice his English with Albert and me. After Albert's death, Alex dropped in more often, and his visits always cheered me. He talked about his students and how he taught them English, about his family in Havana, his friend who had gone to Miami, and his own restlessness. All the time, he'd be fixing my sewing machine, or the kitchen clock, or the gas stove. He managed to get materials to do all the maintenance that we had gotten lax about. He took me to the doctor, did the shopping, cooked the meals we shared.

When I went to the hospital for a kidney operation, I asked Alex to stay in the house, and he agreed. When I came home, he stayed on and took care of me, the house, everything.

I knew Alex wanted to get out of Cuba, and I was the only person who could help him. I had always said I'd never leave the Isle, and I meant it. All my memories were there. Then I realized, yes, I had wonderful parents and a wonderful husband. Now I have Alex. I'd have nobody if I didn't have him.

So we began to plan a short trip to the States, without telling anybody—not even Peggy—that we were going to stay. I held a valid U.S. passport, but Alex needed permission from Cuban immigration officials and a visa from the U.S. consul in Havana to accompany me. He got an affidavit from the hospital saying I could not travel alone in my condition. He also got special permission from the ministry of education to take the trip. Then he filled out all the forms, had interviews with the appropriate officials on both sides, and tried to allay their suspicions. Finally, after six months of waiting, everything was approved for us to leave on December 2, 1987. Alex picked up the visas and our tickets. I was so relieved when I saw them that I began laughing and crying at the same time.

We packed our bags, called a taxi, and locked the door of the casita with my life's treasures inside. I thought I was going to faint as I walked down the steps, but I couldn't show what I was feeling. No one knew we weren't coming back. We were just going on holiday. When we were inside the taxi, I bowed my head to hide the tears.

I don't like Miami. It's so busy and noisy here. There's so much violence, hatred, and drugs. Neighbors don't even greet each other. I don't think I'll ever feel I belong here. I miss my casita, I miss my Cuban friends, and I especially miss Peggy Rice, who has been like a sister. I used to get spells where I wanted to go back, but fortunately I've gotten past that. My life in Cuba is over now, and I couldn't go back. I wouldn't have anyone or any place to go back to.

DISAPPEARING LANGUAGES

Lydia McPherson, whose parents immigrated from Jamaica, was born on the Isle in 1932. She grew up speaking English and knew all the other English-speaking residents, including the Sundstroms.

Lydia McPherson

All the Americans have gone now. The last one to leave was Mrs. Sundstrom. She loved Cuba very much. I don't know why she left and never came back. Well, it wasn't her idea. She was taking care of a young man, and he wanted to leave. She never wanted to leave Cuba—never—and she was well attended and very comfortable all the time. Everybody loved her and treated her very well. She had a kidney operation in the hospital here. You know that these major operations—heart, kidneys, eyes—

*are all free. And although she didn't have any relatives on the is-
land, she had a big family visiting her in the hospital.*

*Everything's different now. There are so many people on the
island, and we are all so busy that we don't always have time to
visit these old friends. But when we see each other, it is the same
love, the same feeling as always. Time passes, maybe a month,
three months, or more, and we don't see each other. There's too
much work and studying and all. It's not the same leisurely way
it used to be.*

*My mother and father met here and married and had six chil-
dren. I have a sister who has lived in Miami for years, and my
oldest brother lives in New Orleans. I have never traveled out of
Cuba. My father was a farmer, but the farm was out of town,
and we lived in Gerona because there were public schools here.
We went first to a school with a Jamaican teacher and then to
the Lutheran Church School. Then we learned Spanish in the
public school. I didn't go on studying because I lost my mother
when I was eleven years old, and I was needed at home to take
care of my younger sisters. I was married when I was nineteen,
to a Cuban, and we had six girls. Then we separated, and now
I'm married to a Jamaican.*

*I always spoke English to the children, but my Cuban husband
didn't speak English. The children understand it, but they don't
speak it well. At first they didn't like to and all that foolishness.
Then they just wouldn't put it into their heads. Afterwards, my
oldest daughter went to night school for English, but she didn't
want to be a linguist. She wanted another profession, and now
she's a laboratory microbiologist.*

*All of my children work here on the Isle. The oldest is thirty-
five, and the youngest is twenty-five. The second oldest is an
analyst in the food industry. One of the twins is an office worker,
a secretary; and the other teaches nursery school. My daughter
Lydia, my namesake, is a supervisor at the grapefruit processing*

plant. My smallest daughter is a production worker in a dairy combine.

I've been working in this motel for nearly ten years, since 1981. I'm the only one in the establishment who speaks English, and we have a lot of English-speaking people coming around: some Canadians, Germans, Africans—it depends. So I can help them out here in the gift shop, or at the desk, wherever English is necessary.

Before the revolution, I wouldn't have had this job. In the fifties I waited table in a restaurant, and the only other thing I could do then was be a housekeeper for somebody else, like my mother was. I wouldn't say I felt discrimination when I was young, because on this island even the foreigners didn't discriminate. The Americans didn't discriminate. It was like a big family, and the Americans who lived here were like family with the other foreigners and with the Cubans.

But the opportunities weren't the same then. My children have had the opportunity of studying whatever they wanted, no discrimination and no pay difference, because they all grew up in the revolution. Cuba has problems, of course. I think all countries have problems. But we all have the same care, rich or poor, and you know we have these big operations and everything is free. You don't have to pay anything in a hospital, so that's a great advantage. Before, you were like a beggar, and you had to give all kinds of details about your family to get free treatment.

Mosako Harada

Our twelve children went to school here on the Isle, and four of them went on to high school and university in Havana. One of our daughters married a Japanese diplomat there, and he took her back to Japan with him. No communist country for him or his wife, he said.

A few years ago, Kesano and I went to Japan to see our daugh-

ter and all the relatives we hadn't ever visited together. Everybody insisted on entertaining us, and I discovered what hard work a vacation trip can be. We were exhausted when we left there and very happy to come back to the farm.

The other children are here in Cuba, some in Havana and some on the Isle. They're all married and have children. I can't even keep track of how many grandchildren and great grandchildren we have, but I know not one of them speaks a word of Japanese. The grandchildren oblige you to speak Spanish. They don't answer me when I speak Japanese, and they aren't interested in any of our customs either.

Eduardo Hanzawa

Hanzawa, Harada, Ogoshi, Miyasawa, Oyiyama—a dozen or so immigrant families founded the Japanese community and established the Japanese Association. I'm a grandson of the first Hanzawa who came to the Isle in 1926. The surviving family elders speak only Japanese. I've always spoken Japanese with them and Spanish with everyone else. My parents knew Spanish, so I learned that even before I started school in the seventies. I finished high school here on the Isle and studied engineering at the University of Havana. English was part of the curriculum, and that came in handy when I met my girlfriend, who's Danish. With my little bit of English and her little bit of Spanish, we manage to communicate when she comes to visit me.

I'm a member of the Hanzawa family cooperative, but I don't work in the fields. I work as an engineer at the water filter plant. In the older generations, women and men worked in the fields, but the young are all educated, and very few work in agriculture. The cooperative is managed by the associates, and some of them supervise and participate in farming activities that require additional hired help. Everyone speaks Spanish, of course. The cooperative is very well organized and managed. It is self-sufficient

in all kinds of vegetables, also pigs, goats, chickens, cattle for
meat and milk—the surplus milk goes to the day-care centers. It
has been profitable for three years straight, since 1993, and
that's good for everybody.

The Japanese Association doesn't have much to do. It was or-
ganized by the original family heads to keep the Japanese fami-
lies in touch and promote their mutual interests. Now it meets
infrequently and just for social get-togethers.

Like the Japanese immigrants, the English-speaking immigrants
also lived in their own communities and spoke their own language.
Frequent intermarriage among first-generation Jamaican and Caymanian descendants kept English alive even after the American exo-
dus. In families with names such as Ebanks, Elliot, Ferguson, Jackson,
McPherson, Swevy, Powery, or Yates, the older people still speak English by preference; but their children and grandchildren—like the
Japanese—learned to think, speak, read, and write in Spanish at
school. By the third generation, all were more or less Cubanized.

Peggy Rice's granddaughter Margarita got what she has called "the
English treatment" from both her mother and her grandmother. English was part of her home environment, and she learned to speak it
fluently, with a softened version of Peggy's clipped British accent. At
the same time, Spanish was all around her, in her mother's rapid-fire
fluency, in the neighborhood, at school. It eventually became her first
language, the one she speaks and writes most easily.

Margarita Valdés

After I had Jackie in 1977, I studied some more. I finished four
grades of night school, studying English from six to eight in the
evening. They gave me my diploma for qualifying. And maybe I
could have worked at the Colony [Hotel], with the foreigners
and all that. But I decided to stay home and take care of Gran,
because the Colony is a long way off, and she'd be all alone and

we didn't have much family. I studied a little more and got to the eleventh grade, and then I dropped it.

Jackie needed more from me, too. She was having trouble in school. She didn't feel good where she was, and I thought it would be best to change her while she was still interested in studying; and that's what we did.

I figured it was Jackie's time. I had to take care of her. My time was past. Maybe later on I can study some more because now she's in high school, and she's not here all week, just weekends. She likes the Tupac Amaru and she gets good grades—better than I did. Jackie's very pretty, and she's popular with her school chums, but she's not seriously interested in any of the boys, and I'm glad of that.

I finally found Julio. We're not married legally, but we've been living together for three years, and I think it's been better in a way than being married. We get along with each other. He helps us a lot. He's very fond of Gran and of Jackie. And, well, my idea of a family is actually coming true.

It's a nice house we have here, and I like my yard with all my chickens and ducks. This has been my home all my life. I'm happy here. Sometimes I don't go anyplace for weeks. I don't work. I don't shop. Julio does the shopping. Julio does everything. I take care of the house: the cooking, the washing and ironing, the cleaning, and all of that stuff. It seems like quite a bit sometimes.

I suppose it's good to get out and meet people and get more of a notion of things. Jackie's growing up now, and there's no entertainment, no theater, no big places where young people can meet and know a little of everything. Maybe I'd like a change for her. But if it was for me, I'd stay here all my life.

On the Isle of Youth, everybody speaks Cuban Spanish. Even the foreign students from Angola, Bolivia, Benin, Burundi, Cape Verde, the Congo, Equatorial Guinea, Ethiopia, Guinea Bissau, Guinea, Kampuchea, Mali, Mozambique, Namibia, Saharawi, Sao Tomé y Príncipe, Santa Lucía, Seychelles, Surinam, Yemen, and Zimbabwe had to learn Spanish as a prerequisite for their other subjects; and the Bolivians and Nicaraguans had to become attuned to a cadence quite different from their own Spanish.

The first group of foreign students came from Angola—more than 2,000 seventh graders who took over four junior high schools—and a smaller group of Mozambicans followed within weeks. They were the majority from 1977, when the program began, until 1997, when it ended.

In magnitude alone, the foreign students' program was impressive, but there were also great differences in the background and preparation of students. They were assigned to junior high schools by nationality and spent the week studying in their own schools. Sports competitions and cultural events brought the schools into contact from time to time, and the students often went into town on weekends. Contact with island residents was quite limited until students reached the senior high school level, where education was more integrated.

Over twenty years, some 34,000 students from 117 countries were graduated in Cuba, most of them young men. On the Isle, in the higher level of the Teachers' Training College for the 1995–96 school year, a total of 1,367 Zimbabwean, Angolan, and Cuban students and a few Namibians were enrolled, but the breakdown by sex was revealing: Zimbabwe, 41 women out of a total of 954 students; Angola, 61 women out of a total of 263 students; Namibia, 3 women out of a total of 13 students; Cuba, 140 women out of a total of 160 students.[18]

Many of the graduates from the schools on the Isle were successfully applying their skills and knowledge in their own countries when

Isle of Youth Foreign Scholarship Students Graduated as of July 1997

Country	No. Students	High School	University
Angola	3,688	3,418	270
Benin	40	40	
Bolivia	2	2	
Burkina Faso	197	197	
Burundi	4	4	
Cabo Verde	286	286	
Cambodia	8	8	
Congo	340	340	
Dominica	1	1	
Ecuador	4	4	
Ethiopia	649	649	
Ghana	310	310	
Grenada	1	1	
Guinea (Equatorial)	15	15	
Guinea Bissau	641	641	
Guinea (Republic)	12	12	
Guyana	1	1	
Haiti	17	17	
Korea (North)	79	79	
Lesotho	7	7	
Madagascar	1	1	
Mali	16	16	
Mozambique	1,647	1,647	
Namibia	463	463	
Nicaragua	1,023	1,023	
Panama	4	4	
Sahara (Polisario)	289	289	
Santa Lucia	1	1	
Sao Tome y Principe	36	36	
Seychelles	4	4	
Sierra Leona	2	2	
South Africa	2	2	
Sudan	186	186	
Surinam	2	2	
Uganda	1	1	
Yemen	104	104	
Zimbabwe	1,179		1,179
TOTAL	11,262	9,813	1,449

Mined Diplan Libreta No. 2

the program officially ended. A few of them (all men) returned to Cuba in July 1997 to celebrate the Fourteenth World Festival of Youth and Students. They told how they had arrived on the Isle of Youth, homesick and nearly illiterate in their own languages, to be welcomed by warm and patient teachers; and they spoke of their careers back home in medicine, teaching, and a variety of technical fields (*Granma*, 31-7-97).

This noble and generous program was fraught with complexities that ranged from sheer numbers to the students' varying national origins, primary schooling, and lifestyles. They all began as seventh graders, but some of the students from the former Portuguese colonies communicated chiefly in one or another tribal dialect when they started learning Spanish. Unfamiliar with their new environment, they stuck with the classmates they knew, sometimes acting aggressively against others. Manuel Fernández Fala, a twenty-year-old Angolan graduate of the Animal Husbandry–Veterinary Polytechnical Institute (equivalent to eleventh grade) and outgoing Student Council president in 1995, remembered what it was like when he was a seventh grader:

Manuel Fernández Fala

There were lots of fights by nationality, and, since there were always more Angolan students, it seemed like the Angolans were the main troublemakers. The seventh graders are the worst. They're young and undisciplined. I was like that too when I came. I rebelled at everything and wrote my family that I was coming home; but my parents said, no, I was here to study and that's what I should do because it was my responsibility not to let them down. I thought about it a lot and realized they were right. Then, by the time I got into the Polytechnical, I was more mature. I could analyze things better.

We had a serious disciplinary problem a while back, again with some Angolan students. A few of us got together and threw a birthday party for a friend. It wasn't a party for everybody, just for a small group. But some of the others decided to crash it. When they tried to push into the room where we were partying, we barred the way and explained that it was a private party. They were mad as hell and left. A little while later they came back, two of them armed with long neon lightbulbs. Before we knew what was happening, their lead man cracked a lightbulb over a friend's head and bloodied him pretty badly. I grabbed the other one and disarmed him, and the rest of them fled. The leaders of that attack were expelled from the school and from Cuba.

We've had other disciplinary problems, too: kids sneaking back into the food line before everyone was served—that's serious, you know, because it means that someone goes without dinner— lack of respect for teachers, and absences in the field. The Student Council is responsible for solving these problems. We try to handle each case individually and reasonably, and, since we're students just like they are, they usually listen.

We have to set an example. I mean, we have to be disciplined, and we have to tackle all the hard jobs first. For instance, we organized a volunteer brigade to clear the fields around the school of brush to make charcoal, which we sold to buy ice for the icebox so we could keep the fish and chopped meat for a day or two after it arrived (fish is delivered on Wednesday, chopped meat on Thursday, bread and sweets come daily). Then we planted the cleared fields with garden vegetables for our own consumption. We solved several problems for the school with that project.

We organize sports for competition by nationality; we set up the guard duty (10 P.M. to 3 A.M. night duty, 3 to 6 A.M. student guard). We make games, like checkers and chess pieces, out of wood and cardboard scraps; we have birthday parties and so on.

Alfred Ackom, of Ghana, and José Dina, of Mozambique, graduated with Manuel Fernández and served as vice presidents on the Student

Council, which included a representative of each country and met weekly to analyze problems and report to the school leadership. The three student leaders agreed that the school was well organized and the curriculum practical. Ackom planned to work in animal husbandry in Ghana but was considering further education, perhaps in the United States, where an uncle teaches college. Dina hoped to work in a provincial veterinary program, but was worried about military service requisites. Fernández was concerned about the volatile situation in Angola and the prospects of military conscription. "The government could pick me up on the streets of Luanda, just like that," he said, "and unless my family can bail me out, off I'll go."

On the eve of their departure from the Isle of Youth, these three were feeling somewhat nostalgic about teachers and fellow students they might never see again, the more so perhaps because they were among the last in the program. Many of the sixty ESBEC buildings were already empty by the end of the 1995 school term.

It was in the 1980s that increasing numbers of foreign students began entering senior high schools, technical institutes, and college branches for specific studies without regard to nationality. As they moved into higher education, they became more demanding. For the first time, there were student protests by foreign teenagers who wanted access to the consumer goods available only in a few dollar stores set up for diplomats and foreign residents. The foreign students were added to that list, and special certificates were issued to them in the amounts transferred to the Cuban bank by their families or governments. Meanwhile, it was illegal for ordinary Cuban citizens to have dollars. Some of the students received as much as $100 a month in certificates redeemable in government-controlled dollar stores, restaurants, hotels, cabarets, and on Cubana Airlines. The measure was profitable for the banks and for the foreign students. Inevitably, it engendered black marketeering and prostitution, both of which escalated elsewhere in Cuba with the increase in tourism.

When the foreign student program ended in 1997, two of the

former ESBEC schools had been converted into community housing for agricultural workers and their families. A dozen were functioning as local junior and senior high schools, technical institutes, and university branches. Guards were posted in the remaining empty buildings (around forty) to prevent further vandalizing until their future use, or destruction, could be determined.

In the 1998 school year, nearly 12,000 elementary, 4,000 junior high, and 2,000 senior high and polytechnical students (almost all Cubans) were enrolled in schools on the Isle of Youth. Of the eleven ESBEC or junior highs, eight were rural and three were urban, while all eight senior highs were rural (three pre-university, three agricultural, and two economy institutes).

GOLD ON THE ISLE

The island's gold lies in its citrus orchards—grapefruit, oranges, limes. It takes three years for a grapefruit seedling to grow and yield fruit, but the plant may go on producing for forty or more years—as was true of some 600 hectares of orchards the American settlers laid out in the early years of the century. Between 1960 and 1980, nearly 45,000 additional hectares were planted, and the 1987 harvest totaled 150,000 tons, of which 120,000 tons (mostly grapefruit) were exported to socialist countries (*Granma*, 5-4-88). Thousands of students took part in pruning and fertilizing the orchards and harvesting the fruit for local consumption, but professional workers selected the grapefruit designated for export.

Grapefruit was incorporated into the island's cultural life when the first Grapefruit Festival was held in January 1983, at the end of the harvest. For several years, this lively, cosmopolitan celebration was an annual affair, with African, Latin American, and Japanese cuisine, music, dance, and crafts contributed by residents and foreign students.

Sorting grape-
fruit at the
packing plant

In 1987 optimism about increased citrus exports was so great that a harvest of 400,000 tons was predicted for the year 2000 (on the assumption that irrigation would be extended to increase yields in the then nonirrigated orchards that made up 30 percent of the total).

Cuban engineers also aired an ambitious project to drastically cut shipping costs by building a deepwater dock in the extreme north of Siguanea Bay, joined by bridge and causeway to the northwest coast of the Isle (*Granma*, 17-8-89). Thus the fruit could be trucked directly to the export carrier and would no longer have to be towed by barge to some other port for final shipment. It was a revival of the deepwater dock project begun on Siguanea Bay in 1910, except that the 1989 version never left the drawing board.

With the 1990s came the collapse of the socialist bloc, dashing hopes for economic improvement in the foreseeable future. The citrus export market evaporated, and there was no Soviet oil to fuel the diesel-run motors that pumped the irrigation system.

In the early nineties, there were still students around to help harvest the grapefruit that could no longer be marketed. The 1993 harvest was so big that a cottage industry was created on the Isle to produce grapefruit sweets of all kinds—the state provided the sugar and found a neighborhood *gestor*, an official promoter-salesman for homemade concoctions. This was the alternative to grapefruit in its natural state, which Cubans tend to reject not only because it's too tart, but also because it is said to lower blood pressure dangerously. As the island drink of hospitality, though, grapefruit juice is acceptable, especially when laced with rum and sweetened with sugar.

Meanwhile, Pole Isla, a Uruguayan company with Chilean capital, signed a five-year agreement in 1991 to process and export Isle of Youth grapefruit and by-products, with the Army of Working Youth (EJT)[19] providing militarized agricultural labor. It was the first joint venture in citrus (two others followed on the main island), and its Chilean managing director seemed confident of increasing annual exports—and profits. Not only was the Isle of Youth grapefruit top quality, he noted, but it was also "the first to arrive on the European market and this puts us in an advantageous position" (*Granma International*, 27-9-95).

In 1995 number 49 of the ESBEC schools was converted to housing for citrus workers and their families. A community in itself, the prefab, renamed Marmolsol, has 100 apartments with one, two, or three bedrooms, one bathroom, kitchen, and living-dining room. Public facilities include a grocery, post office and public telephone, day care and primary school, and a medical post. The apartments are given in usufruct as long as the worker remains contracted to the citrus plan. A second ESBEC has since been converted for another project of "sustainable" agriculture on the Isle.

However, in 1996, when the Pole Isla agreement on Isle of Youth citrus expired, it was not renewed. With no foreign investors, no foreign markets, and no foreign students, citrus seemed to have dried up. In 1997 the grapefruit yield had dropped to 14,000 tons, and some of the orchards had been abandoned or cut back to plant other food crops. Yet, just a year later and without foreign investment, citrus was beginning to recover, this time with Valencia oranges in the lead. As a start, 225 new hectares were equipped with modern irrigation systems and planted with oranges. A harvest of some 35,000 tons of citrus was promised for 1998–99 (*Granma*, 12-10-98).

Tobacco, which American settlers grew so successfully in soil very similar to that of Pinar del Río's *vuelta abajo* across the channel, is now being grown again on the Isle at an experimental tobacco plantation that produced its first crop in 1997 and began hiring for increased production a year later. Interestingly, women are more stable in these jobs than men, according to their employers.

Food crops for local consumption have priority in the strategy of sustainable agriculture, but quantities have been less than sufficient. Analyzing the most serious problems on the Isle as of April 1998, members of the Political Bureau of the Central Committee of the Communist Party of Cuba cited, among others, the failure to meet production plans in tomatoes, potatoes, bananas, melons, and other fruits and vegetables; and the continuing illegal slaughter of cattle (*Granma*, 1-5-98). Yet with the winter harvests of 1998–99, food shortages were not a major complaint.

THE MILKY WAY

Pineros look back with nostalgia to *las vacas gordas* (fat cows), as they call the prosperous decade of the eighties. Those were the years when their own real, live fat cow produced so much milk that she became a local, national, and even international celebrity. On January 3, 1982, when Castro visited Ubre Blanca (White Udder) at Dairy Farm No. 5 in La Victoria, the cross known as F1 (three parts Holstein, one part Cebú) must have made a commitment to the *Comandante*, for she soon surpassed all records, producing 27,674 kilograms of milk in a year and 110 liters in a single day.

Ubre Blanca even became a sightseeing option for visitors, who were given all the ruminative details of the star's life, down to the number of bites of grass per minute she consumed (65) and the amount of supplementary food she received daily (22.5 kg.). Nor was she a slouch in reproduction; impregnated by embryonic transplant, Ubre Blanca gave birth to five calves in one pregnancy, which seemed to augur well for the future. But the well-kept scientific secret was that Ubre Blanca was a one-time genetic phenomenon, and none of her offspring would match her productive records.

After the death of the mighty milch cow, *pinero* sculptors Avelardo Echevarría, Luis Ruíz, and the late Pablo Porro Gener carved a life-size image of Ubre Blanca in the Isle's white marble to be pastured permanently and prominently as a symbol of the Isle's agrological advances. Echevarría visualized the figure at the center of a composition that would show other genetic and scientific accomplishments. Some considered the statue a whimsical but misleading representation of island progress: what about grapefruit, or schools, or ceramics? There was also the question of selecting an appropriate location for the statue.

While discussion of scope and venue continued, Echevarría and Ruíz stabled the monumental figure in a corner of their workshop. Visitors were welcome to view Ubre Blanca there, surrounded by the artists' more modest expressions of socialist realism: ceramic boxes holding six quarts of milk, ceramic sacks bulging with potatoes at points that evoked a female figure, marble farm tools in phallic forms, polished wooden fruits, and an enormous fiber-covered wire mobile representing the countryside itself.

Today the marble memorial stands, appropriately, at the entrance to the town of La Victoria, close to the dairy farm where Ubre Blanca set her phenomenal records. She is remembered as a unique champ in a cattle breeding strategy that daily produced pasteurized milk for all the schools and *bodegas* on the Isle—until her death and the special period put an end to the imported nutrients, fertilizers, insecticides, and phytosanitary products that nourished the *vacas gordas*.

INDUSTRIALIZING THE ISLE

Between 1978 and 1983, gross production in food processing and the fishing industry more than doubled and so did the generation of electricity. The Isle produced all its own construction materials—from cement to marble—and most of the furniture for new educational, medical, housing, commercial, and recreational facilities.

The kaolin processing plant that Ernesto Ché Guevara inaugurated in 1964, when he was Cuban minister of industries, was expanded and modernized in 1978 to permit a production of 30,000 tons annually, used to make tires, medicines, cosmetics, paper, and industrial ceramics of every kind, but especially tableware—predicted to become the top marketable product that would outstrip even grapefruit and its by-products.

Harriet Wheeler's pottery crafted with local kaolin in the twenties and thirties was the historical inspiration for the fledgling industry. Although her house in Santa Barbara had been eliminated by the reservoir, her kiln remained as her monument, and some of her decorative and utilitarian pieces were still around long after her death. Over the years, Sylvia Baker, Edith Sundstrom, Peggy Rice, and other friends continued to use the distinctive, durable bowls, pitchers, plates, and cups she had given them. Later, a few pieces found their way into the ceramics wing of the Model Prison Museum, alongside works by modern potters whose ceramic murals added color and movement to public parks and buildings.

In 1970 the first ceramics factory was built, and a small vocational school began training machine operators for the incipient industry. The production included sets of glazed tableware, unadorned or decorated only with a colored band.

That same year, Daniel García, a recent graduate of the famous San Alejandro Art School in Havana, came to the Isle to teach art.

Daniel García

I came to the Isle to do a year's social service, and I've been here nearly thirty years. For twelve years I taught art at the art center of the vocational school. Many of my former students are professional painters and ceramists, and others continue painting as a hobby. By custom, it seems to me the best way to teach art is by observing nature. That way you can explain colors, perspectives, depth, materials.

The first course I taught was just a year, and, when it was over, some of the students wanted to continue painting for their own enjoyment. So we formed an art club. Some of the founders of that club are still members, and, of course, their work has improved a lot over the years. Every two weeks, we go out to paint landscapes or some public building, like a market. With the administrator's agreement we draw up a design and spend a few hours brightening up the walls and enjoying our group work. The club has a dozen or so members, and they're all amateurs. They work as teachers, technicians, photographers, planners, architects, housewives, and paint on alternate Saturdays.

Later, the art courses at the vocational school became more formal and complete. Some of the graduates are now art teachers, and several of those who learned ceramics by doing voluntary works in the ceramics factory became designers for the industrial pottery produced on the Isle.

Angel Norniella Santos

*I came to the Isle in 1964 because there were more jobs here
than in Oriente, where I was born. I found work in a machine
shop, first as an instruments mechanic and then in the design department, making wooden models of the parts. It was very inter-
esting work; I learned a lot about wood; and since I didn't have
much to do after work, I began studying English, French, and art,
after Daniel García founded the art center in the vocational
school.*

*The first art class began in 1970, but I didn't know about it be-
cause I had gone to Oriente for vacation. When I got back, the
registration was closed. I begged Daniel to let me in, but he said
he couldn't because he didn't have enough workbenches. "No
problem," I told him, "I'll make my own bench." But he told me
he needed several. Where I worked, I could get the wood, so I
made all the benches he needed. It was the same with the tables
... the shelves ... and finally he let me take the course.*

*That's where I began to do ceramics, because Daniel and some
of the other teachers and students would spend weekends in the
ceramics factory painting the dishes with a glaze of floral and
landscape designs that were very fresh and decorative and very
durable, too. But we were night students with daytime jobs, and
we could only work weekends. We couldn't keep up with the production, so the position of decorator was created, with specific
criteria, and was first filled by students from the art school.*

*When Erich Honecker, then president of the German Demo-
cratic Republic, visited the ceramics factory in 1978, what interested him was the artistic decoration, and from that visit came
the technological aid and equipment to set up a series of ceramic
workshops on the Isle.*

Amelia Carballo Moreno

*After I graduated from the San Alejandro School, I came to the
Isle in 1972 to work with Daniel García at the art school. It had
already been decided to establish the ceramics industry on the
Isle, and the art school added a new dimension to the Ceramics
Technological Institute when some of the professors and students
began applying design motifs to the tableware. That's how most
of us were introduced to ceramics, and it became clear that it was
our artistic touch that gave the tableware its distinction. It made
a real difference in the East Germans' decision to help expand
the industry in 1978 by setting up ten ceramics workshops on
the Isle, each of which could develop a separate line and give jobs
to local residents. At the same time, some of our artists were invited to Germany for study and training. The idea was for the
artists to continue creating designs in the Experimental Ceramics Workshop that Angel and I struggled so hard to establish.*

*We would test designs, glazes, colors, and marketing needs in
order to give each ceramics workshop a well-designed line of
production. Unfortunately, it didn't work out that way; the idea
of creating good designs for industry became distorted. So we decided that, if we were going to do ceramics, we had to do it in our
own individual workshops, and we set up Terracota 4.*

Angel Norniella

*The Experimental Ceramics Workshop was supposed to be a cen-
ter where artists and designers would develop materials, colors,
and forms, test their findings in the market, and incorporate the
results into the industry. Instead, it turned out reproductions for
gifts and souvenirs, thereby compromising industrial development on the Isle.*

*The materials of the Isle do not produce porcelain, but a very
resistant pottery, and a good designer can combine color and*

form in attractive patterns. However, the policy was wrong, and many of these factories are now closed. They can no longer compete. The reasons are multiple: imports are costly, the budget is low, they aren't profitable, and they have no market. If they had functioned properly, if there had been some foresight, they could be producing and selling their specialty, each one with its own line of production. The buyers would be mostly hotels that purchase complete sets of tableware. If the four-and five-star hotels import porcelain, there are plenty of lesser category hotels that could use the Isle's pottery, but they have to count on purchasing complete sets, on continuing production. The domestic market is unlimited, but it has never been tapped. Now it may be too late.

Through most of the nineties, the ceramics industry on the Isle was limited to sanitary and electrical fixtures. Whatever remained of the decorated tableware produced in the eighties was on sale in a few dollar stores in Havana. Amelia and Angel, two of the chief designers for that experiment, got together with other artists to form Terracota 4 in Nueva Gerona. In 1996, seeking broader exposure and a market, they moved Terracota 4 to Old Havana, the art center of Cuba.

Paralyzed for five years, Cuba's major factory for the production of ceramic tableware reopened on the Isle in January 1998, with the announcement of lower costs, higher production, improved quality, and, especially, experimentation to attain white clay (the production is largely cream colored), better mixtures, and glazes using local materials.

THE QUALITY OF LIFE IN 1990

In the spring of 1990, only the tip of the iceberg that lay ahead was visible. Cuba tightened its belt to withstand Eastern-bloc shortfalls and shored up its defenses as American warships maneuvered in Caribbean waters. The Communist Party of Cuba drew up an agenda for its upcoming Fourth Congress.

"The perspective our Party offers the people today is neither cata-strophic nor pessimistic," read the "Call" published on the front page of the Isle of Youth daily *Victoria* for May 3, 1990. Nevertheless, there would be greater sacrifice in the name of "peace, liberty, and the right to continue the battle for the well-being, happiness, and betterment of all Cubans." Reassuringly, the front page also carried a photo of the upbeat concert by Los Van Van (Go-Go) held the night before in the main square of Nueva Gerona—a "soul-warming evening," Shug described it.

We had just arrived to spend several weeks on the Isle as temporary residents in a centrally located apartment that Magaly Reyes of ICAP had arranged. We were able to travel all over the Isle because we had our own transportation and could purchase gas in dollars. Accompa-nied by Rufus, the long-haired dachshund, I had driven our Lada onto the ferry in Batabanó early one morning and driven it off in Nueva Gerona that same afternoon. Juan Colina met me in his Polski, showed me to our quarters—a sunny three-bedroom apartment with a tiny front balcony—and helped me unload the Lada. Bill, inclined to seasickness, flew over the next day.

Compared to Havana, Nueva Gerona was an oasis of prosperity and activity at that moment. In front of the hospital (doubled in size since the sixties), heavy traffic consisting of horse-and mule-drawn carts, bicycles, motorcycles, cars, buses, trucks, ambulances, and taxis passed in both directions. The hospital marked the town's northern border in 1959. The cemetery beyond it was outside city limits. By the begin-ning of the nineties, these institutions of life and death were com-pletely surrounded by new prefab housing developments. Most of the buildings were five-story walkups with two comfortable apartments per floor. Litter-free front lawns, connecting walkways, and gardens indicated civic concern.

Thirty-Ninth Street, Gerona's main thoroughfare, abuts the hospi-tal at its northern end and runs south past the post office, bank, hard-ware and dry goods stores (then displaying a pitiful selection of ra-

Shoe-shine corner in downtown Gerona

tioned housewares and textiles), the popular Cochinito restaurant specializing in pork, bookstores, galleries, offices, cafeterias, a bakery, houses, and office buildings.

Thirty-Ninth street forges history at Main Square—called Arms Square in colonial times, when its surrounding buildings were the Protectorate, Military Headquarters, and the Catholic church Nuestra Señora de los Dolores. In 1957 Father Guillermo Sardiñas left that parochial parish to join Fidel Castro's guerrilla struggle (the only Cuban priest to do so) and was eventually promoted to *comandante*. Main Square is where Castro outlined development directives for the Isle in 1959, where the public trial of two young murderers was held in 1967 (the shade trees from which some residents viewed the proceedings have since been cut down), where art students draw and paint in the former Protectorate, and where, in 1990, the Van Van blasted secular sounds across a dancing crowd to Los Dolores church and the site of Evangelina Cossio's 1896 rebellion.

At the Thirty-Ninth Street bakery, long loaves of crunchy bread came out of the ovens in the morning and again in the afternoon. It was first come, first served, as much as you wanted at twenty centavos a loaf (about ten cents). By mid-morning, a street vendor would appear with his cart, grilling seasoned pork and onions and serving them on a roll. Soon, another vendor would appear with ham and cheese sandwiches, then another with sweets. This mobile fast food was an out-service of the state-run restaurants.

All the *bodegas* supplied their regular clients with basic rations at controlled prices. Nonrationed products such as live fowl, yogurt, butter, eggs, and plenty of fruits and vegetables were available at public markets. In the parallel market, what Harry Koenig called the *abusadora* store, the prices were higher, but the products included tinned meats and fish, juices, tomato sauce, cooking oil, and even detergent to supplement rations. All three shopping options were run by the state, and payment everywhere was in Cuban pesos.

Sufficient distribution outlets and supplies made for a much shorter queue than in Havana. That, in turn, meant that everyone was pleasant, and nobody tried to jump the line. The markets were clean, and some had cheerful fruits and vegetables painted on the walls, a project organized by artist Daniel García and his enthusiastic amateur art club members.

A single dollar shop was open to foreigners only. It was stocked with clothing, tape recorders, snacks, rum, coffee, cigarettes, and other consumer goods that foreign students could buy with certificates. Jeans and underwear were popular purchases for resale or bartering.

One Sunday, we all drove out in the country to have dinner at El Mesón, a former Methodist church with a choir loft turned into a bar, and tables and chairs replacing pews in the nave. There was a ten-minute wait for a table, and the head waitress reluctantly admitted the irresistible Rufus on my oath that he wouldn't bark or move from under our table. While Bill and I savored beef stew and cold beer, our darling dachshund curled up quietly at my feet. After we finished, the head waitress motioned us out to the back patio, where Chef Alberto had a meat-and-bones feast for Rufus as a reward for his good behavior. El Mesón won our three votes as the best restaurant on the Isle.

When I went to see Peggy, she gave me mangoes; Sylvia insisted I take a pineapple Ramón had brought over; one of Annie and Rulle's sons appeared with a round ripe cantaloupe; Harada took me out to the fields where Kesano was selecting fruit for the market and picked me the sweetest watermelon I've ever tasted. Mangoes, melons, pineapple, and watermelon were all plentiful that spring.

Travel in the northern part of the Isle is unrestricted, but the underpopulated south is a military zone, and a permit is required to cross the Lanier Swamp, which separates the two areas. The swamp is a forest reserve and natural habitat of the Cuban crocodile (*Crocodilus rhombifer*), now cultivated at a breeding farm on the northeastern edge of the swamp. (Cuba's only other crocodile crèche is in the swampland of the Zapata Peninsula near the Bay of Pigs.) With our permit in order and a driver from the Cuban Institute of Friendship with the Peoples ICAP as guide, we set off early one morning for Cocodrilo, which old-timers refer to as Jacksonville. At the checkpoint, an over-zealous young guard refused to let us through because the dog's name wasn't on the pass. Unruffled, the ICAP driver asked me how to spell "Rufus" and wrote the name down. "Just a little oversight," he told the guard, who smiled and waved us on.

We drove along the two-lane dirt road through marshy terrain to a picturesque seaside village where sun-bleached wooden cottages on stilts and blooming bougainvillea bushes border the azure water. Though Spanish is gradually taking over, English with a Cayman lilt is still spoken in this town named for Maud Jackson's father-in-law. We visited Maud; stopped by to see Dick Hydes, an old friend of the Jackson family; dropped in on relatives of Rulle and Annie Ebanks; wandered into a store with empty shelves ("deliveries late this month," we were told); watched kids swinging in a playground on the dunes; then drove along the coast to the fishing cooperative at

Cocodrilo Point and on to Caleta Grande, where the big turtles and other chelonians are bred. In a grove of pines overlooking the sea, we opened our cooler and picnicked on the sandwiches and refreshing orange nectar we had brought along. There were no problems on the way back to Nueva Gerona, and the trip seemed a lot shorter.

The most festive happening of the month was the parade of white-frosted, pink-trimmed cakes emanating from the Thirty-Ninth Street bakery on a particular Saturday afternoon. Flour (imported from eastern Europe) was in short supply on the Isle, but the pastry cooks of Nueva Gerona had promised 10,000 cakes for Mother's Day on Sunday, May 15. They stretched the flour with wheat roughage; beat in the required shortening, sugar, and eggs; and poured the mixture into round and square pans. After the cakes were baked, the decorators took over. Every cake was finished with a rosy *"Felicidades"* to congratulate Mama.

Our stay on the Isle ended that night. Bill's return to Havana by plane was no problem, but my departure, scheduled for midnight, was complicated by the regulation mandating separate cargo and passenger travel at night, for safety reasons. Thus the Lada had to be freighted aboard the slow old *Palma Soriano* that had brought us to the Isle, while Rufus and I returned on the newer, faster *Isla de la Juventud* passenger ferry, in its enclosed cabin lounge. To reach the lounge, I had to maneuver up a rope stairway from the main deck with a trusting deadweight dog under one arm and a heavy duffel hanging from the opposite shoulder. My cool traveling companion found a comfortable place under my red plastic lounge seat and settled in.

In the glare of fluorescent lights and the blare of recorded music, the passengers smoked and socialized. Uniformed students chattered about the next day's classes in Havana. Two families were returning to the capital after a week's visit on the Isle. An elderly couple in the care of a solicitous middle-aged daughter was traveling to Havana for medical treatment. *"Merienda,"* blared the loud-speaker, and everyone lined up for what turned out to be a glass of watery lemonade and crackers. I drank some water from my thermos and poured a little into a dish for Rufus. The lights were dimmed, and we all dozed.

The *Isla* pulled up to the wharf in Batabanó just before dawn, and the rope staircase was even harder to negotiate going down. Then, with Rufus on leash, we walked the length of the dark wharf to the terminal, where most passengers boarded buses for Havana. For those with cars aboard the *Palma Soriano*, there remained a mile walk through a black curtain of mosquitoes to the cargo dock, where the boat pulled in two hours later. Just twelve hours after leaving Nueva Gerona, we arrived home. It takes about half as long on the hydrofoil, including Havana-Batabanó by bus. The plane trip is twenty-five minutes, with check-in an hour before departure, and costs forty dollars round-trip.

PEGGY AT NINETY IN 1991

On Peggy's ninetieth birthday, September 28, 1991, I flew over for the day, leaving at 7 A.M. and returning at 7 P.M. She knew I was coming to take her to lunch at the Colony, but I was glad I hadn't specified the time.

There were no taxis at the airport—an ominous sign—but the bus took me directly to the Cubana Airlines office in Gerona, where I had to confirm my return flight. There I got a zoned taxi that took me to the out-of-town terminal, where I joined the *cola*. After a two-hour wait, I squeezed into a taxi with three other passengers and persuaded the driver to deliver them first, pick up Peggy at her house in Patria, and drive us on to the Colony Hotel. The choice of the Colony was calculated; its dollar restaurant would be sure to have food, unlike the pesos restaurants in Gerona, and it also had a dollar gift shop.

Peggy was all dressed up for the outing and walked the few steps from door to taxi supported by her cane and her granddaughter. She

Family transportation

poured herself into the back seat, and I climbed in beside her. Shug closed the door, and Peggy waved goodbye as if we were going on a long trip, then chatted cheerfully during the ride.

When we reached the Colony, the driver handed her down, and she walked the few steps to the door, leaning slightly on her cane. As we entered the lobby, Peggy's gaze faltered at the expanse of marble before her. She managed to cross it, somewhat shakily, and sat down gratefully in the restaurant but said she had no appetite. Finally, in the face of my entreaties and those of a doctor friend who came over to greet her, Peggy ordered chicken soup and took a few sips.

After lunch, we went into the gift shop, where she was the center of attention as she selected her birthday presents: a carton of imported cigarettes (she immediately lit one), shampoo, hand lotion, a bottle of wine for Shug and Julio, and chocolates for Jackie. Her best birthday present was at home, and I handed it to her after we got back. It was a pretty flowered housecoat that Edith Sundstrom had sent her through me.

"Now wasn't that sweet of Edith," Peggy said with tears in her eyes. "I know she misses me the way I miss her. We've been best friends for years. She left because Alex wanted to leave, but she won't come back, of course. Alex treats her like a queen. She has everything she wants—except me. She'd like me to come visit her, but I can't travel. I won't be going anywhere any more."

Peggy drank the strong black coffee Shug handed her and lit another cigarette while she showed me pictures of Edith and herself when they were younger; of Edith and Albert with Edith's parents; and all her own family photos of a lifetime. Then the neighbors came in, and it was time for the birthday cake. Peggy looked around, smiled wanly, and lit still another cigarette. What was she thinking about on her ninetieth birthday? As I kissed her goodbye, she said urgently: "I must tell you. I read my bible every night, and it says the world is going to end in a great famine."

That was the last time I saw her alive. Early in the morning of April 24, 1992, Peggy Rice died peacefully in her sleep. She was buried that afternoon, a few hours after I arrived on the Isle. With Shug, Jackie, and other friends of the family, I followed the hearse to the town cemetery just beyond the hospital. It crossed my mind that Peggy might have preferred to be buried in the American cemetery, where she had pointed out the tombstones of old friends one afternoon. Yet, as the casket was lowered and covered with wreaths, it seemed appropriate that the island-born granddaughter and great-granddaughter of this last British immigrant should bury her in the traditional cemetery of ornate arches and monuments where her daughter had also been laid to rest.

THE SPECIAL PERIOD

Peggy's vision that the world would end in famine seemed dangerously close to fulfillment when she died. In the officially declared "special period in time of war," food production suddenly became the top priority on this largely agricultural island.

The only crop in surplus in 1993 was grapefruit, and that was the last big citrus harvest of the nineties. Mosako Harada—the farmer who had always grown the biggest, the juiciest, and the tastiest watermelons on the Isle—had very few that year. "Melons need five kinds of pesticides, along with fertilizer, and I had none of either," he said sadly.

Harada recalled the time Castro came to taste his famed watermelons back in the seventies. "I wasn't here, and nobody could find any ripe melons. When I got back, I poked through the fields and found fourteen ripe ones, so I loaded them in the truck and drove them up to Júcaro for Fidel. Good thing he didn't come this year."

Harada complained about stray cattle from the state farm next door trampling his peppers and tomatoes. When he reported the problem, authorities told him there was no wire to repair the fences. Over the next few years, stray cattle became such a problem on the Isle that Minister of the Armed Forces Raúl Castro called a meeting of Politburo members in February 1995 to discuss bovine destruction of citrus groves and how to contain the animals, as reported on national TV.

Broken fences, along with fodder shortages, proved to be a boon to cattle rustlers on the Isle and in the cattle-raising provinces of eastern Cuba. The animals were privately rounded up for illegal slaughter, and the meat was sold on the black market at a time when no rationed beef was available to the population. Some of these prospering cattle thieves were eventually caught by the TV camera, but the problem was a serious one all through the nineties. In December 1997 an open letter was addressed to the CDRs (Committees for the Defense of the Revolution) in Havana (of which the Isle is a Special Municipality), condemning the widespread door-to-door sale of black-market beef at two dollars a pound.

Raising chickens, goats, and even pigs in the backyard or kitchen patio became commonplace on the Isle. If the animals were outside, they had to be penned and guarded by a fierce dog to prevent theft; in an urban apartment, they could lead to serious hygienic problems. One might evade the health inspector with a couple of chickens, but a pig—*cochino*—is readily detectable by sight and odor. Necessity being the mother of invention, the municipal delegates of Popular Power came up with a safe, hygienic, and collective solution to the private ownership of a hog: the *cochiquero*, or community pen, where the *cochino* can be safely boarded, fattened, and slaughtered at the owner's expense.

By 1992 the wonderful fresh-baked loaves of bread we had purchased two years earlier had disappeared. With the collapse of the Soviet bloc, Cuba—which grows no wheat—had to import flour from the capitalist area, or do without. Soybean flour was substituted, but neither taste nor texture matched what *pineros* had grown accustomed to munching. Several bakeries, including one where Shug's Julio worked, were closed.

Especially difficult for Cubans used to frying almost everything was the drop in monthly rations of cooking oil from a liter to a half pint—when it appeared. "They say that's all there is," Harry Koenig grumbled, "but peanuts grow very well on the Isle, and sunflowers don't need any care at all. Why don't they plant them so we can have enough oil?"

Cooking fuel was another problem. In town many apartment dwellers had gas stoves, but the bottled gas that fueled them had practically disappeared. Out in Santa Barbara, Sylvia Baker did her essential cooking—boiling the milk Ramón brought over once a week from his farm and making an occasional cup of coffee—"on a little kerosene stove, and always before dark, when the peak-hour blackout starts, and you can't do anything." Shug and Julio alternated between gas and kerosene for cooking, but sometimes had neither, and Julio was forced to make charcoal. For a while, charcoal became the main cooking fuel, even in the schools, "and that means lots of trees are cut to burn down the wood for charcoal," Harry commented. His brother

Willy concurred, adding that he was paying thirty pesos (about $1.50) for a sack of charcoal, "and it's hard to come by at that." Fuel, along with food, had become the bottom line of daily life on the Isle.

With wood in short supply, the dismantling of Edith Sundstrom's bungalow in 1995 should have come as no surprise. I was an unsuspecting witness to the beginning of that project when I happened to walk by the house, saw the door ajar, and nervily looked in. The furniture was gone, and two men seemed to be raising some of the floor boards. "Making repairs?" I asked with a smile, and they nodded uneasily. When further questioning produced blank stares, I assumed they either didn't understand my Spanish or had been sent to do specific work without knowing the purpose—as is often the case. So I left, certain that the Sundstrom house was being restored as a modest memorial to an earlier period.

Instead, it was torn down, plank by plank until nothing was left standing except the brick chimney. Rumor had it that the finished pine floor beams were stored in somebody's garage, and that the wooden planks were used to make charcoal. The only verifiable fact was that it happened. *Y no pasó nada* (and nothing happened), as the saying goes. Andrés Fernández Soto, who had helped build the bungalow and had painted it every year while the Sundstroms lived there, said the vandalism occurred in two phases: "First they stole all the furniture and, when the house was empty, they knocked it down to the foundations. Bad elements, you know, will take advantage of an empty, unguarded house."

While the Sundstrom house was being pulled down, Virginia Baca Baca's new house out in Los Colonos was going up. Her son had been able to purchase the materials and hire labor to help him build it. That in itself was an opening for private initiative in the nineties. Cement blocks, tile floors, an inside bathroom—the new house seemed grand to Virginia, who had raised her family in the small wooden structure next to it and thought she might just continue to live there.

As she talked, she was interrupted by incoming calls on the commu-

Seaside playground in Cocodrilo

nity telephone. She is the operator who takes all the messages for neighbors during the day and monitors their outgoing calls from 5 P.M. on. Everybody knows the hours, and Virginia Baca Baca knows everybody's business in Los Colonos, where the community phone, electricity, and a few new houses with indoor bathrooms are the main improvements since 1960.

Power blackouts were institutionalized in 1992 (four to eight hours on alternate days, respecting the twice weekly evening soap operas). Residents adjusted to this severe cutback as if it had always existed. Magaly Reyes, Popular Power delegate from the biggest electoral district on the Isle of Youth, was frank in her assessment of the energy shortage as "something that can't be solved right now, so we have to cope with it in other ways . . . cut back as much as we can with scheduled blackouts and fuel-free transportation . . . step up our use of alternative energy sources such as windmills and solar panels . . . develop a consciousness of saving and conserving, of producing more with less."

The first tentative use of alternative energy on the Isle was announced five years later. "Gas Sparks Joy in Cocodrilo," read the headline (*Granma*, 8-5-97) announcing the installation of new stoves and 100-pound tanks of gas to fuel them in all seventy houses in Cocodrilo, replacing traditional charcoal and kerosene burners. In addition, the first solar panels had just been installed in that remote town to guarantee continuous electricity at the local medical post.

The third solar stove donated by German friends of Cuba to nursery schools on the Isle was unloaded at the ICAP office under the supervision of Magaly Reyes in January 1999. These same friends, she explained, invited a technician from the Isle to Germany to learn how to assemble and eventually produce these stoves on the Isle to guarantee alternative energy for kiddy lunches.

Generation of adequate low-cost energy for the entire Isle was promised for late 1999, with completion of a high-tech thermoelectric plant constructed by the Panamanian enterprise Genpower Cuba S.A. at a cost of $5 million, to be amortized within five years (*Juventud Rebelde*, 7-2-99). How better to celebrate the millennium than by reducing blackouts to a historical reference!

MORTALITY

In general, birth rates are decreasing in Cuba, and the population, which reached 11 million in January 1996, is aging. If this pattern continues, one in four Cubans will be over sixty by the year 2025 (*Granma International*, 28-2-96), and the Isle of Youth itself will be graying.

Between 1991 and 1995, six older voices on the Isle were silenced by death: Rulle Ebanks, Peggy Rice, Kesano Harada, Sylvia Baker, Willy Koenig, and his older brother Harry Koenig, the last American resident of the Isle of Pines and Youth.

Because of their advanced ages, they could be expected to figure in the general mortality rates for the Isle, which showed a slight increase over those five years: from 4.5 per thousand inhabitants in 1991 to 5.1 per thousand inhabitants in 1995 (in Cuba as a whole, the figures rose from 6.7 in 1991 to 7.1 in 1995).[20]

At the other end of the scale, infant mortality rates dropped from 15 per thousand live births in 1991 to 10.8 per thousand in 1995 (in Cuba as a whole, they fell from 10.7 in 1991 to 9.4 in 1995).[21] Suddenly, in 1997, infant mortality jumped to 12.7 on the Isle, the highest anywhere in Cuba. Health officials quickly acted to reverse the trend and, by the end of 1998, reported a reduction to 5.4 per thousand live births, the lowest in the country.

This speedy recovery was achieved by direct attention and follow-up through the family doctor network. These doctors now cover 98 percent of the population, working out of neighborhood medical posts staffed round the clock. They have office hours and make house calls, following up on pregnant women from conception to birth, treating minor injuries and illnesses, and summoning hospital ambulances for emergency service. They also organize donors for the mobile blood banks that rotate through the neighborhoods, a service that has increased blood donations to one out of every eight adults.

This community network has reduced concentration on the hospital as the focal point for health care at every level, and, according to the chief surgeon there, medical technology and resources can thus be concentrated on those who need hospitalization. A thorough overhaul of the hospital and its medical equipment in 1997–98 resulted in repairs, replacement of equipment and supplies, a complete paint job, and upgrading of sanitary and service standards. The entire staff received new uniforms, and 400 protective pads were donated for hospital beds, as gifts from friends abroad organized by ICAP's diligent Magaly Reyes.

Said Juan Colina, following an operation and two weeks of hospitalization in 1998, "Isora didn't have to bring me anything from home because the hospital provided everything. Even the food was good. The wards and bathrooms were as immaculate as the main reception

hall. The medical staff, doctors and nurses, knew what they were doing and did it with devotion."

In-patients usually receive the appropriate medication for their
condition, but out-patients often have difficulty filling a prescription
in the local pharmacy, and across-the-counter medicines such as aspi-
rin, vitamins, or eye drops are not to be found anywhere. People have
turned to home remedies based on green medicine and alternative
therapy ranging from massage and exercise to thermal baths.

In La Fé, doctors, naturalists, and community activists organized a
Popular Council to rescue the famous Santa Rita mineral springs.
With pick and shovel, local residents removed the earth and mud that
for so many years had blocked the springs and filled the pools. Doctors
and thermal scientists once again analyzed the physical-chemical
properties and pronounced them super-sterile, with radioactive, pro-
tein, antibiotic, amino acid, and gaseous components. While no resources were immediately available to rebuild the installations, 2,000
people immersed themselves in the healing tepid springs during the
first month they were open in 1999, and more than a few claimed
immediate relief, mainly from arthritic and skin afflictions (*Granma*,
10-2-99).

RETURN TO THE CHURCH

On Sundays the main social activity on the Isle revolves around
the churches—as it did in prerevolutionary years. Both Catholic and
Protestant churches began to revive in the early nineties, after the
Party gave its official blessing to the practice of religion. *Santería*,
which developed as the religion of spiritual survival for blacks living
in the slavocracy of the main island, has only shallow roots on the Isle,
and its practitioners are few. The nineteenth-century Catholic church
of Nueva Gerona, Nuestra Señora de los Dolores, shares its pastor
with another municipality. Two Protestant churches have maintained
services since the early days of the century. Today, the Methodist

church has a loyal congregation composed mostly of older women and children. The Church of God, largely attended by Jamaican and Cayman residents in Sylvia Baker's time, is now the strongest Protestant—and evangelical—presence.

With national offices and two churches on the Isle, the Church of God is directed by the Reverend Samuel Contino, native born. The church missionary board in Anderson, Indiana, has provided financial aid to expand church facilities and services in Nueva Gerona and to reopen a temple in Santa Fé. Medicines and toiletries have been distributed from the church, while equipment and supplies have been donated to clinics and schools. Religious classes, sports activities, and services are well attended. Reverend Contino is an empathetic and charismatic person with an excellent understanding of relations between the Cuban state and the churches. The Church of God appears to be in the vanguard of the Protestant religious renaissance on the Isle, while other denominations long absent from ecclesiastical activities are now pressing to recover their status and their properties.

As the distance between church and state narrows, prerevolutionary street and town names with religious connotations have been officially accepted. Thus La Fé is again Santa Fé, and La Demajagua[22] has reverted to Santa Barbara. *Pineros,* though, are *pineros,* even those born on the Isle of Youth.

ALIENATION AND RESILIENCE

Individual responses to the economic crisis of the past decade run the gamut, and Cuban investigators acknowledge not only a return to religion and a strengthening of family solidarity but also social alienation, a higher incidence of alcoholism and aggressive behavior (often combined), passivity to the point of depression, and other psychological problems.[23] On the Isle of Youth, the incidence of personal violence is twice as high as the national average, according to a reliable source.

At the same time, the crisis has engendered a forthright and ongoing polemic on the destructuring and restructuring of Cuban society. Everybody blames, complains, and proposes: "Silence is not the pervading theme in contemporary Cuba; Cubans have never been silent. They openly voice their opinions in the range of formal and informal contexts."[24]

The economic free fall on the Isle of Youth reached bottom in 1995 and 1996, with a very small upturn noticeable by 1997, which continued unevenly through the rest of the century. The prognosis is that "Cuban living standards won't return to the 1989 level until 2014."[25]

Nevertheless, Cubans are a resilient lot, and the lot of more than 80,000 *pineros* is by no means desperate. With a consolidated service sector and a militarized agricultural workforce, the population is guaranteed a minimum standard of living that includes food, education, and health care. In other Third World countries, such things might be a dream, but not here. The middle-aged adults on the Isle are the youth of the sixties and seventies who worked and sacrificed for that and more. Their children and grandchildren, raised on the Isle, take those social benefits for granted and want something for themselves.

José Antonio Mayal, Jackie's father, was no longer required to support his twenty-one-year old in 1999, but he had a thirteen-year-old still eligible for child support out of his low wages as a night watchman. José Antonio is a native *pinero*, born in 1957 and educated in the Isle's new boarding schools. He attended the first elementary boarding school that opened in Santa Fé, Amistad con los Pueblos, in 1961 (elementary boarding schools have since been phased out as both costly and problematic) and finished two years of junior high before he quit school to work in a warehouse.

José Antonio Mayal Arteaga

I've been working since 1973, and I have nothing, nothing at all, not even a place of my own. I live alone, in a friend's house. On the Isle, everything is difficult. I don't see any improvement. If

things are a little better here, they're a little worse there. You
spend all your time working. Yes, the children have free educa-
tion. Health care is free for everyone. There are many good
things. But you can never get ahead. No matter how hard you
try, no matter how much you work, no matter what efforts you
make, you'll always stay right where you are. Nothing changes.

I've never had anything, and I never will; since I'm not an en-
gineer or an architect or a doctor, I'm even worse off. Especially
in this special period when there aren't any jobs, even for those
who have a career. If you study and graduate as an engineer, for
example, you're not going to work in agriculture. Yes, there are
jobs in agriculture, but lots of people won't take them. It's not
easy.

With more schooling and career focus, others of his generation are
better off. Of Isora and Juan Colina's three daughters, one is a nurse,
one a museum archivist, and the third glazes pottery reproductions at
the Experimental Ceramics Workshop. Magaly Reyes's agronomist
daughter has become a computer engineer at the Isle's Academy of
Sciences, one son is an art teacher, and the other son is biding time as
a chauffeur while looking for a job where he can pursue his career as
an audio engineer. They, too, however, live with parents or friends and
own nothing more than a bicycle.

TOURISM

When the dollar was legalized for Cubans at the end of 1993, it was
already required tender for foreigners patronizing any state-run establishment. At one time or another, I had stayed in most of the small
peso hotels: Rancho del Tesoro, Bibijagua, and Las Codornices (where
Lydia McPherson worked). Like all the other (mostly Cuban) guests,
I tolerated cockroaches and mosquitoes, bad food and dirty table-
cloths, blaring music and cold showers. By 1992 none of those accom-

modations could be relied on for food or water, and most were "closed for renovations." To pick up the dollar slack, the Gaviota tourism group, reportedly launched with military backing, opened a new dollar hotel near the airport. Villa Gaviota offered comfortable, moderately priced accommodations ($25 per night for a double room), good food, and a rental car with driver.

On a bright Sunday morning, we drove down to Punta del Este, at the eastern tip of the south shore. There, above the pristine beach, stand the awesome caves that sheltered Indian canoeists thousands of years ago as they paddled through the Caribbean. On the ceiling of what has been designated Cave Number 1, the primitive Guanahatabey Indians painted concentric circles in red and black, representing the phases of the moon, in order to calculate the periods favorable for navigation. The caves are pierced by natural light that also reveals serpents, human figures, and crosses drawn on the walls by the pre-Columbian visitors. The woods around the caves are full of honeybees and infested with mosquitoes. Nobody seems to know how to protect the former while eliminating the latter, so both buzz on.

Down on the beach, a family of three lolled in the shallows, and a van pulled up on the sand to unload a group of student naturalists equipped with butterfly nets, binoculars, and cameras. Between the caves and the beach, surrounded by trees and brush, was a new wooden vacation cottage built by a Cuba-Basque joint venture. It was the beginning, and end, of a 750-room project to bring ecological tourism to the Isle of Youth. Within a year, the investors pulled out—driven away by the mosquitoes?—leaving Cuban archaeologists and meteorologists to monitor the mysteries of Punta del Este.

By early 1999 the buzz of major tourism investments on the south shore was back. How can it be otherwise along that virgin coast, no matter how firmly environmentalists argue against it? Meanwhile, cruise ship lines contracted to bring some 120,000 passengers to Cuban ports during 1999. Havana is the principal port of call, and Punta Francés, at the western tip of the Isle of Youth, is the complementary virgin territory projected for 70 percent of this specialized tourism (*Granma*, 12-12-98). Mongo Rives and his Tumbita Criolla met the first cruise ship arrivals at Punta Francés, playing their *sucu-suco* music.

To preserve the coralline habitat here, the cruise ships tie up to an offshore buoy in waters 200 to 300 feet deep, and the passengers come ashore in small boats to lie on the beach or view the moving submarine paradise. Punta Francés has fifty-six marked scuba sites with such evocative and literal names as Tunnel of Love, Witch's Cave, Sunken Ship, Coral Funnel, Queen's Garden, Pirate's Anchor, and fifty others. Underwater adventures are led by internationally registered scuba guides from the Colony Hotel, which provides all collateral safety measures. The area is considered one of the four best scuba sites in the world.

The number one tourist pole on Los Canarreos Archipelago is Cayo Largo, ninety kilometers east of the Isle of Youth. Cayo Largo is one of Cuba's major dollar-earning resorts. A tiny key with no resources of its own, it imports absolutely everything and mostly from abroad—even though the Isle of Youth, in the same municipality, should be able to provide all construction materials, from cement and tiles to precious woods and high-quality marble. "This territory should direct more of its efforts and activities to hotel development on Cayo Largo del Sur," the Political Bureau Commission stated in its report of the April 1998 meeting on the Isle of Youth, "which would also have positive repercussions for the economy of the country and the Isle of Youth in particular" (*Granma*, 1-5-98). In other words, the Isle could become an important point for stopping Cayo Largo's hard currency leakage.[26]

Nevertheless, the complexities, rigidities, uncertainties, and pressures of a mixed economy in flux operate against contracting for domestic production. The wholesale buyer (foreign or national) finds it easier, safer, and sometimes cheaper to import from abroad (*Trabajadores*, 9-2-98).

Already, many of the personnel working in Cayo Largo tourism come from the Isle of Youth. Recently, the Bamboo, a small hotel outside Gerona, was remodeled to function as a tourism training school that can provide upgraded services in this developing enclave of Cuba's main industry.

Tourism is still a minor concern of environmentalists on the Isle and one in which they can only advise what, where, and how to build. Their chief concerns are preserving rare and indigenous species of chelonians, crocodiles, parrots, and other birds; reforestation and protection of natural resources; and fire prevention.

In May 1998 more than 600 firefighters fought for three days to extinguish a forest fire around Los Indios, thirty kilometers southwest of Nueva Gerona. Because of the drought, the blaze advanced rapidly toward a 1,000-hectare ecological reserve and habitat for the Cuban parrot *(Amazona Leucocephala palmarum)*, then in its mating season; the sandhill crane *(Grus canadensis)*; and other rare birds, reptiles, and plants. The wooded reserve is bordered by a protective barrier of evergreen eucalyptus—grown from seedlings planted in the sixties—pines, and pot-bellied palms that separate it from an open savanna inhabited by cranes. The fire was extinguished with little damage to the fauna.

On a soggy January day eight months after the fire, the parrots and cranes were in hiding, and the savanna bloomed with creepers and bushes that become tinder-dry under the burning summer sun. According to environmental specialists,[27] the life cycle of this savanna depends on fire to create the oxyacid sandy soil used in construction materials, and it is precisely the burned-over area that attracts the cranes. A savanna fire sometimes fizzles out on its own, but it has to be watched and controlled to prevent destruction of the fauna and their forest habitat. Parrots lay from one to four eggs a year and seldom produce in captivity. Cranes mate for life, usually lay two eggs annually (of which only one hatches), and almost never produce in captivity. Both are considered endangered species, as is the Cuban crocodile, bred only on the Isle of Youth and the Zapata Peninsula; and the sea turtles protected at the Caleta Grande chelonian breeding station on the south coast.

The only parrot to reveal its colorful plumage that day was Margarita's Perico, whose masculine name stuck even after it laid an egg (that never hatched). Margarita acquired Perico in 1995, after the death of Peggy's parrot Coty, also female. She expects Perico to live into the first decade of the twenty-first century on a healthy diet of fruit, guava seeds, corn kernels, and peanuts. The parrot is especially crazy about peanuts and gurgles happily at their appearance, but when she's hungry, Perico calls crossly and insistently, "Margarita, come here!"

THE QUALITY OF LIFE IN 1999

Margarita Valdés hasn't been called "Shug" since her grandmother died in 1992, ending a three-decade relationship of mutual affection and care-giving. At fifteen, shortly after her mother's death, Margarita gave birth to Jackie, who was fifteen when "Gran," as they both called Peggy Rice, died. Even as she mourned, Margarita celebrated her grandmother's long life and her peaceful death at ninety-one. Jackie, however, was angry and rebellious. Rejecting maternal solicitude, she ran away from home. A distressed Margarita broke up with Julio, looked into trading her house for two smaller places, then realized she simply couldn't give up her animals and garden. She persuaded Jackie to move back with the promise of dividing the house. "So we can live our own lives," Jackie said meaningfully after it was done.

Yaqueline Mayal Valdés was born October 16, 1977, in the modern Nueva Gerona hospital. She grew up under the permissive tutelage of her great-grandmother and her mother (whose early marriage turned into early divorce—but no hard feelings) and continued to see her father, who lived nearby. Scholastically and socially, she adapted to the strictures of boarding school and graduated from high school at eighteen.

By the time this generation X princess with curly black tresses and luminous brown eyes turned twenty-one in 1998, she had her own working papers and a devoted, hard-working husband who was frequently out to sea catching lobster for export. Osmel fishes with his crewmates in a boat rented to them by the national fishing industry, which also purchases their catch in dollars. Jackie is a licensed English teacher who doesn't want to teach ("too much hassle and, besides, I don't like kids"). She's a natural candidate for the tourism training school, but hasn't applied: "You have to be a cadre with all kinds of recommendations, so I wouldn't be accepted." For the moment she's a full-time housewife whose care-giving extends to her guinea hens and a husband, when he's home. She doesn't smoke or drink and almost never goes out. Hers is a life of idleness with just one addiction: the evening soap opera.

The main part of the house is occupied by Margarita and her new husband, Mario, plus Perico and three cats that wander in and out. In the backyard are chickens and ducks and multiplying guinea pigs. Chained near the doghouse is a big, ferocious-sounding Doberman type. The grounds are as well kept as ever, but the house needs repairs, paint, and new screening. Margarita pointed to the bare walls and sparsely furnished parlor. "I've sold some of Gran's pictures and furniture," she said simply. "That money and the food packages and cash from Mario's mother in the States are what we've been living on. I've never worked, and the wages Mario would earn as a mechanic aren't worth it. Occasionally he repairs somebody's iron or washing machine and that's it."

Margarita and Mario are among the estimated 5 million privileged Cubans[28] who receive remittances from relatives abroad to acquire the food, clothing, and household goods that, just ten years ago, they could purchase with Cuban pesos and their ration book. No wonder Cubans quip that it's either *dólares o dolores*, greenbacks or grief.

Margarita Valdés

Mario and I get along well, even though everything is such a struggle and we have so little money. Then there was the expense of dividing the house, and that's when I sold some of the furnishings, because Jackie was still single and jobless. I wanted to do it, not just because she insisted, but because I realized she needed her own space.

I want Jackie to get a job. I don't want her to be a housewife all her life like me. She needs to get out and do something for herself, not just sit back and wait for her husband. Osmel is a good person, kind and very hardworking. He loves fishing and earns good money. He and Jackie get along fine now, but they're both young, and marriages can break up. Jackie should have her own independent life and earn her own money. The discipline of a job to replace the discipline of school would do her good. It was different for me. I had Gran to take care of and my daughter, too, which meant the house and the animals as well. Jackie doesn't have those responsibilities. She has a high school degree and a diploma to teach English. She could work in tourism, and the new school would be a good place to start. I'm trying to persuade her to apply there, but of course she has to make up her own mind.

Without illusions or great expectations, Jackie is simply waiting. When I asked her what she wanted most for the millennium, she was straightforward: "I want to have a good job and live alone." Then she retired to her room and tuned in her TV to dream in color with the evening soap opera.

Epilogue

DAUGHTER OF THE CARIBBEAN

I

Solitude and secrecy were the primacy.
Next the dance of corals
that lived their spiraled voyage
to achieve—over centuries—
the marvel of a birth
on the Caribbean surface.

Coasts ever newly formed
cradled by swelling waves—virgin—
tracing the silhouette of mystery

eternally gray
eternally renovated—and renovating—
in the face of the rocks.

It was a passionate Guanahatabey
who drew love in circles
of blood and minerals.
In the hollow of his caverns
magic appeared.

And later, the deluded admiral
who noted in his logbook the discovery
of cranes, white and gigantic,
like monks.

And what's to say of the corsairs
and pirates? It was their hideout
and retreat.
They planted gold in its waters
as in a natural safe.

Today the Tumbita Criolla
performs for visitors and immigrants
of all colors and nations
while, with naive vanity,
the woodland musicians
match the transcendental
rhythm of a sucu-suco.

But the Isle continues to be
everyone's and no one's!

II

The renowned and the rare I came to know
in the green wisdom of its red mangroves.

The spray of its beaches—
voluble as females—
flirted with my adolescence,
and the sands of blackest marble
guided my bare feet
to hidden places perfumed by the woods
of all the sunken galleons.

Isle of incredible flora—
pines and pot-bellied palms—
special creature!

Now I comprehend the motives
of that Indian,
of Christopher Columbus,
of the corsairs and pirates,
of Mongo Rives and his Tumbita Criolla,
of the visitors and immigrants.

I perceive the light in their fascinated eyes,
as they, like me, lose themselves
in delicious fantasy
seeking the lost trail
of an eternal youth
filled with illusions
like this Isle,
incomparable daughter of the Caribbean.

Roberto Díaz Blanco* (Trans. Jane McManus)

*Roberto Díaz Blanco (born in Havana, 1963) spent his adolescence on the Isle of Youth as a student and writer for Radio Caribe. Now living in Havana, he wrote this poem after a visit to the Isle in 1998.

Notes

CHAPTER 1

1. Investigating an outbreak of yellow fever among U.S. troops stationed in
   Cuba in 1900, a team headed by U.S. Army Surgeon Walter Reed proved
   Cuban physician Carlos Finlay's mosquito transmission theory. Mosquito eradication and sanitary procedures followed, and a vaccine was
   developed to control the disease before construction of the Panama Canal
   began in 1904.
2. Rodríguez et al., *Latifundismo y especulación*, 4.
3. Guantánamo Naval Base, though militarily and politically obsolete, is
   still held in lease by the United States in spite of persistent Cuban demands for its return.
4. Le Riverend, *Economic History of Cuba*, 224.
5. Rodríguez et al., *Latifundismo*, 5.
6. Ibid., 6.
7. Wright, *Isle of Pines*, 32.
8. Wright, *Cuba*, 321.
9. Freeman and Nearing, *Dollar Diplomacy*, 180.
10. Wright, *Isle of Pines*, 88.
11. *Isle of Pines Appeal*, 11-5-12.

12. Approximately 150,000 to 200,000 crates of tomatoes, peppers, and eggplants were exported each year in the period 1910–1927. See Rodríguez et al., *Latifundismo*.

13. *Isla de Pinos y las companies [sic] norteamericanas*, 7–10.

14. Ibid., 10.

15. Browning, "Isle of Pines," 1–10.

16. Published in 1883, a half century after piracy in the Caribbean was outlawed, Stevenson's *Treasure Island* describes an imaginary place that resembles the southern part of the Isle of Pines, but also has many characteristics of an island in the South Pacific.

17. Roosevelt was elected vice president under President William McKinley in 1900, became president following McKinley's assassination in September 1901, and was elected president by a landslide in 1904. Wood, promoted to general, cleaned up Santiago and replaced Brooke as commander of the occupation forces in Cuba.

18. Alvarez Estévez, *Tratado Hay-Quesada*, 49–50.

19. Torriente y Peraza, *Mi misión en Washington*, 87.

20. Almost as soon as the votes were in, Machado jailed Mella on a false murder charge. When Mella went on a hunger strike, Machado released him to exile in Mexico and, in 1929, hired assassins to gun down the young rebel on the streets of Mexico City.

21. The war and postwar "dance of the millions" in Cuban sugar profits came to an abrupt end when prices on the world market dropped from twenty to three cents a pound in the last six months of 1920. See Le Riverend, 225.

22. Unterecker, *Voyager*, 456–57.

CHAPTER 2

1. Morales, *Situación social*, end table.

2. *Sucu-sucu* or *sucu-suco* is the name of the dance, the music that accompanies it, and the family fiesta where it is celebrated. It developed on the Isle from the influence of the *son* that mariners brought from eastern Cuba and the round dances that arrived with the Cayman Islanders, reaching the pinnacle of its popularity from the 1920s to 1940s. The musical instruments were usually accordion, harmonica, bongo, gourds, and guitar or violin. From childhood, Sonny Boy (born in 1928) played in a group formed by his Jamaican parents and their Caymanian friends. At the same time, Mongo Rives, *pinero* of Cuban and Spanish descent,

was playing with his father's *sucu-suco* group before founding his own, Tumbita Criolla. See Linares, *El sucu-sucu*, 4–10.

3. This was the hurricane of November 9, 1932, classified in Cuban meteorological records from 1800 to 1998 as the worst natural catastrophe in Cuban history, claiming 3,000 victims in Santa Cruz del Sur, Camagüey (*Granma*, 15-8-98). It did not hit the Isle directly, as did the great hurricanes of 1926 and 1944.

4. Roa, *La revolución del 30*, 74–75.

5. Morales, *Situación social*, 13.

6. Guiteras pushed through an eight-hour work law and a minimum wage, cut electric service rates, distributed land, dissolved the political parties that had supported Machado, and demanded abrogation of the Platt Amendment. He also gave his friend Torriente Brau access to the damning testimony for *La Isla de los 500 asesinatos*. When the government fell, Guiteras determined to leave Cuba and regroup for armed struggle, but he was assassinated at his departure point on the Matanzas coast.

7. González Valenzuela, "Isla de Pinos: ¿Tambien un campo de concentración en Cuba?"

8. Colina, "Presidio Modelo."

9. González Valenzuela, "Isla de Pinos."

10. Beals, *The Crime of Cuba*, 378.

11. Medina, "El presidio," 12.

12. Peña Hijuelos et al., *Con todo derecho*, 130.

13. Senator Eduardo Chibás's commitment to honesty and truth presumably led him to shoot himself in the abdomen during his weekly radio program on August 5, 1951, when he was unable to document charges of corruption he had made. He died some days later.

14. Mencía, *Time Was on Our Side*, 17.

15. The dates refer to July 26, 27, and 28, an official three-day holiday in memory of the Moncada attack (26) and its martyrs (27–28).

16. Mencía, *Time*, 68.

CHAPTER 3

1. Armando Hart Davalos became Cuba's minister of education in 1959, later served as minister of culture, and is currently (1999) director of studies on Martí. He is a longtime member of the Central Committee of the Communist Party of Cuba and the Council of State.

2. José Ramón Fernández Alvarez has held many posts, the latest being president of the Cuban Olympic Committee. He is a member of the

CCCPC and vice president of the Executive Committee of the Council of Ministers.

3. Colina, "El Primero de Enero en Isla de Pinos."
4. *Revolución*, 8-6-59.
5. Sutherland, *The Youngest Revolution*, 243.
6. Ibid., 236.
7. *Census de población*, vol. 15.
8. Martin, 1969 interviews.
9. Marin, *Condenados*, 96–142.
10. Sutherland, *The Youngest Revolution*, 222.
11. Mendez, "Historia," 37.
12. Marin, *Condenados*, 345.
13. Telephone interview with Merrill Dodge, August 1997.
14. Peña Hijuelos et al., *Con todo derecho*, 136.
15. Castro Ruz, speech of June 29, 1971.
16. Legendary Peruvian Indian chief. The modern guerrilla movement is named for him.
17. Lutjens, *State*, 117.
18. Elejalde Villalón, director of higher education.
19. EJT is a division of the Revolutionary Armed Forces (FAR) that supplies and administers human and material resources for agricultural plans by contract.
20. *Anuario demografico de Cuba*, 1995.
21. Ibid.
22. The plantation in eastern Cuba where Carlos Manuel de Cespedes freed his slaves and declared Cuba's first War of Independence in 1868.
23. Martín Fernández et al., "La vida cotidiana," 92–98.
24. Bengelsdorf, *The Problem of Democracy*, 179.
25. Mead, "Castro's Successor," 49.
26. Pattullo, *Last Resorts*, 46, considers that "the enclave nature of Cuba's tourist industry has limited that potential."
27. Field trip with José Izquierdo Novelles, specialist of the Environmental Unit.
28. "Cuba: L'Embargo s'assouplit," 16.

Bibliography

Allouis, René, and Jesús Alvarez. "Cocodrilo." *Juventud Rebelde,* 16 April 1969.

Alonso Valdés, Coralia. *Población, migración internacional y desarrollo regional: Una experiencia cubana: Isla de la Juventud.* Havana: Seminar on Population and the New International Economic Order, 1984.

Alvarez Estévez, Rolando. *Isla de Pinos y el Tratado Hay-Quesada.* Havana: Editorial de Ciencias Sociales, 1973.

———. *La "reeducación" de la mujer cubana en la colonia: La Casa de Recogidas.* Havana: Editorial de Ciencias Sociales, 1972.

Alvarez, Guillermo. "Sus lentes hicieron historia." *Juventud Rebelde,* May 1990.

Anderson, Jon Lee. *Che Guevara.* New York: Grove Press, 1997.

Anglo-American Directory of Cuba. 1956–1957 edition.

Anuario demográfico de Cuba, 1990. Havana: Instituto de Investigaciones Estadísticas, 1992.

Anuario demográfico de Cuba, 1995. Havana: Oficina Nacional de Estadísticas, 1996.

Asuntos políticos legajo 97, exp. 33. "Comunicaciones acerca de la fuga de la cárcel de mujeres de la presa política Evangelina Cosio Cisneros 8 octubre 1897." Havana, National Archives.

Beals, Carleton. *The Crime of Cuba.* Philadelphia: J. B. Lippincott, 1933.

Bengelsdorf, Carollee. *The Problem of Democracy in Cuba: Between Vision and Reality.* New York: Oxford University Press, 1994.

Benjamin, Medea, Joseph Collins, and Michael Scott. *No Free Lunch: Food and Revolution in Cuba.* San Francisco: Institute for Food and Development Policy, 1984.

Bonachea, Rolando E., and Nelson P. Valdés. *Revolutionary Struggle, 1947–1958.* Vol. 1, *Selected Works of Fidel Castro.* Cambridge, Mass.: MIT Press, 1972.

Branly, Roberto. *Prosa oral: Anecdotario pinero.* Serie Isla de Pinos 12. Havana: Instituto de Literatura y Lingüística, Academia de Ciencias de Cuba, 1967.

Browning, William. "The Isle of Pines as a Hibernaculum." *Long Island Medical Journal,* March 1910.

Bryan, William S. *Our Islands and Their People as Seen with Camera and Pencil.* St. Louis: N. D. Thompson, 1898.

Burkett, Elinor. "The Last American." *Miami Herald,* 4 September 1988.

Castro Ruz, Fidel. "Discurso en la inauguración de la presa Viet Nam Heroico, Isla de Pinos." *Granma,* 12 August 1967.

———. "Discurso en la Isla de Pinos." *Revolución,* 9 June 1959.

———. "Discurso en la Isla de Pinos." *Granma,* 29 June 1971.

Census de población y vivienda municipio especial Isla de la Juventud. Vol. 15. Comité Estatal de Estadísticas, Oficina Nacional del Censo República de Cuba, 1970.

Clark, Sydney. *All the Best in Cuba.* Rev. ed. New York: Dodd, Mead and Company, 1956.

Colina la Rosa, Juan. "Africa: Isla de Pinos–Isla de la Juventud." Unpublished research paper.

———. "Caimaneros y Jamaicanos en Isla de Pinos." Unpublished research paper.

———. "Cronologia." Unpublished research paper.

———. "Floridianos en Isla de Pinos." Unpublished research paper.

———. "Monologo de la muerte." *Museo Presidio Modelo boletin no. 2,* March 1991.

———. "Presidio Modelo." Unpublished research paper.

———. "El Primero de Enero en Isla de Pinos." *Historia Pinera,* no. 2, January 1997.

———. "La prisión: Resumen." Unpublished research paper.

Colina la Rosa, Juan, Beatriz Gil García, Jorge Pérez Delgado, and Juan Ramón Basco Díaz. *Isla de la Juventud: Informe a la Asamblea Municipal del Poder Popular de la Isla de la Juventud.* Havana: Editorial José Martí, 1987.

Cossio Cisneros, Evangelina. "This Is the Story of My Life Written for the *Journal.*" *American Magazine of the New York Journal,* 17 October 1897.

———. *The Story of Evangelina Cisneros Told by Herself.* New York: Continental, 1897.

Crane, Hart. "Eternity." *Complete Poems of Hart Crane,* ed. Marc Simon. New York: Liveright Publishing Corporation, 1966. Reprinted by permission of Liveright Publishing Corporation.

"Cuba: L'Embargo s'assouplit." *Le Point,* 9 January 1999.

"De la guerra del '95: La evasión de Evangelina Cossia." *La Discusión,* 7 October 1910.

De la Isla del Tesoro a la Isla de la Juventud. Havana: Editorial Gente Nueva, Edición Encilia Saldaña Molina, 1980.

Díaz Blanco, Roberto. "Hija del Caribe." Poem written for this book, 1998.

Dunbar, Virgina Lyndall. *A Cuban Amazon.* Cincinnati, Ohio: Editor, 1897.

England, George Allen. *Isles of Romance.* New York and London: Century, 1919.

Estudio de las perspectivas del desarrollo socioeconómico de la Isla de la Juventud: Aspectos sociales del desarrollo. Havana: Academia de Ciencias de Cuba, 1984.

Estudio demoeconómico municipio especial Isla de la Juventud. Havana: Dirección de Demografía, Comité Estatal de Estadística, 1981.

Frank, Waldo. *America Hispana: A Portrait and a Prospect.* New York and London: Scribner's, 1931.

Franklin, Jane. *The Cuban Revolution and the United States.* Melbourne, Australia: Ocean Press, 1992.

Freeman, Joseph, and Scott Nearing. *Dollar Diplomacy.* 1925. Reprint, New York: Monthly Review Press, 1966.

Gamez, Tana de, and Arthur R. Pastore. *Mexico and Cuba on Your Own.* New York: R. D. Cortina, Garden City Books, 1954.

Garay, Sindo. "Evangelina." *Bohemia* 59 (29), 21 July 1967, 16.

González Laureiro, Julio César. "Breve historia del Presidio Modelo de Cuba." Unpublished research paper, 1994.

González Valenzuela, Bruno. "Isla de Pinos: ¿También un campo de concentración en Cuba?" Unpublished research paper, 1985.

Herrera Sorzano, Mercedes. "Evolución de la apropiación de las tierras y la producción agropecuaria en Isla de Pinos hasta el siglo XIX." Unpublished research paper.

Historia de Cuba. Havana: FAR Dirección Politica, Editorial de Ciencias Sociales, 1981.

Honigmann, Georg. *El Ciudadano Hearst.* Havana: Ediciones Politicas, 1980.

Horrego Estruch, Leopold. *Juan Gualberto Gómez, un gran inconforme.* Havana: La Milagrosa, 1954.

Hunt, Christopher. *Waiting for Fidel.* Boston and New York: Houghton Mifflin, 1998.

Isla de Pinos y las companies [sic] norteamericanas. Havana: Comisión de la Escuela de Historia de la Universidad de la Habana, 1970.

Isle of Pines Appeal. Founded 1904. Published every Saturday by A. E. Willis, Nueva Gerona, Isle of Pines. E. de Laureal Slevin, editor. Nonconsecutive issues from 1911 through 1925 in Municipal Archives, Nueva Gerona.

Isle of Pines (Caribbean Sea): Its Situation, Physical Features, Inhabitants, Resources, and Industries. Washington, D.C.: Division of Insular Affairs, War Department, 1902.

Isle of Pines News. F. J. Reed, editor and publisher. Nonconsecutive issues from 1909 in Municipal Archives, Nueva Gerona.

Isle of Pines Post. Issues of November 1927 and July 1956.

Julien, Claude. *L'Empire Américain.* Paris: Editions Bernard Grasset, 1968.

Lens y de Vera, Eduardo F. "La isla olvidada: Isla de Pinos." *Estudio físico, económico y humano . . . aprobado por el Primer Congreso Nacional de Geografía celebrado en Cuba.* Havana: First National Geography Congress, 1942.

Le Riverend, Julio. *Economic History of Cuba.* Havana: Book Institute, 1967.

Linares, María Teresa. *El sucu-sucu de Isla de Pinos.* Serie Isla de Pinos 31. Havana: Instituto de Etnologia, Academia de Ciencias de Cuba, 1970.

Lismore, Thomas. *The Coinage of Cuba (1870–1953).* Havana, 1955. Reprint, Colorado Springs: American Numismatic Association, 1966.

López Ortiz, F., and M. Ecay y Tovar. *Cuba Motor Touring Guide.* Havana, 1930.

López Pellon, Nivio. *Hablemos de Isla de Pinos . . . y su régimen fiscal*. Havana: Publicidad Guau, 1958.

Lutjens, Sheryl. *The State, Bureaucracy, and the Cuban Schools: Power and Participation*. Boulder, Colo.: Westview Press, 1996.

Marin, Thelvia. *Condenados: Del presidio a la vida*. Mexico: Siglo XXI, 1976.

Martí, José. *El presidio politico en Cuba*. Havana: Ediciones Protectora del Preso, 1938.

Martín Fernández, Consuelo, Maricela Perera Pérez, and Maiky Díaz Pérez. "La vida cotidiana en Cuba: Una mirada psicosocial." *Temas*, July 1996, 92–98.

Martin, Lionel. *El Joven Fidel*. Rev. 2nd ed. Barcelona: Ediciones Grijalbo, 1982.

———. Unpublished interviews made on Isle of Youth, December 1969.

Mead, Walter Russell. "Castro's Successor?" *New Yorker Cuba Issue*, 26 January 1998.

Medina, Waldo. *El presidio que estorba*. Havana: Editorial Lex, 1947.

———. "El presidio se está tragando la Isla." *Cosas de ayer que sirven para hoy*. Havana: Ediciones Unión, 1978.

———. "Evangelina Cossio: Heroina de Leyenda." *Bohemia Año* 26 (March 1949): 6–8.

Mencía, Mario. *Time Was on Our Side*. Havana: Political Publishers, 1982.

Mendez, Tomás León. "Historia del Hotel Colony." *Historiadores Cronistas*, 1. Isla de la Juventud, n.d.

Mesa, Blanca Mercedes, and Antonia María Tristá. *Cuentos, relatos y refranes pineros*. Serie Isla de Pinos 15. Havana: Instituto de Literatura y Linguística, Academica de Ciencias de Cuba, 1967.

Millard, Joseph. "El asombroso rescate de Evangelina Cossio de Cisneros." *Bohemia* 46 (36), 5 September 1954.

Miller, Tom. *Trading with the Enemy: A Yankee Travels through Castro's Cuba*. New York: Atheneum Press, 1992.

Miranda y de Madariaga, Joaquin de. "Ensayo estadístico político y militar de la Isla de Pinos, colonia Reina Amalia, denominada por Cristobal Colón El Evangelista, por los Indios Camarcó." Original manuscript, 1835. National Library of Cuba.

Miró Argenter, José. *Crónicas de la guerra: La campaña de Occidente, tomo III*. Havana: La Moderna Poesia, 1909.

Morales, Salvador. *Situación social en Isla de Pinos antes de la revolución*. Serie Isla de Pinos 27. Havana: Instituto de Historia, Academia de Ciencias de Cuba, 1969.

New York Evening Sun, 26 January 1898.

New York Journal, 23, 24 August, 10–12 October, 17 December, 1897; 9, 13, 18 January 1898.

New York World, 14, 16, 25 January 1898.

Nuñez Jiménez, Antonio. *La abuela, narraciones.* Lima, Peru: Campodónico Ediciones, 1973.

———. *Cuba con mochila al hombro.* Havana: Ediciones Unión, 1963.

———. *Isla de Pinos: Piratas, colonizadores, rebeldes.* Havana: Editorial Arte y Literatura, 1976.

Orovio, Helio. *Diccionario de la música cubana.* Havana: Editorial Letras Cubanas, 1981.

Pattullo, Polly. *Last Resorts: The Cost of Tourism in the Caribbean.* London: Cassell-Lab, 1996.

Pelaez, Yolanda. "Evangelina Cossio." *Granma,* 31 October 1974.

Peña Hijuelos, W. *Memorial Pinero.* Isla de la Juventud: Poligráfico Pablo de la Torriente Brau, 1987.

Peña Hijuelos, Wiltse, Bruno González Valenzuela, Juan Colina la Rosa, Roberto Nuñez Jauma, and Ricardo Pérez Milham. *Con todo derecho Isla de la Juventud.* Isla de la Juventud: Poligráfico Pablo de la Torriente Brau, 1986.

Phillips, Ruby Hart. *Cuba: Island of Paradox.* New York: McDowell, Obolensky, 1959.

Quesada, Gonzalo de. *The Title of the Republic of Cuba to the Isle of Pines.* Washington, D.C., 1924.

Ramirez Corria, Feliberto. *Excerta de una isla magica.* Mexico: Editorial Olimpo, 1959.

"Rebellion in the Isle of Pines." *Literary Digest,* 25 November 1905, 779.

Revista Cayo Hueso, 26 September 1897, 14 July 1898.

Reynolds, Charles B. *Standard Guide to Cuba.* Havana and New York: Foster and Reynolds, 1916.

Rice, Peggy. "My Life So Far." Unpublished diary owned by Margarita Valdés Rice, 1977.

Rives Pantoja, Mariano. "26 de Julio de 1896: Rebeldía en Isla de Pinos." Unpublished research paper.

Roa, Raúl. *La revolución del 30 se fue a bolina.* Havana: Instituto del Libro, 1969.

Rodríguez Calderón, Mirta. "Evangelina Cossio: La muchacha quinceanera." *Bohemia* 59 (29), 21 July 1967, 16–22.

Rodríguez, Delfin, Gloria García, Segundo Pérez, and Jorge Ibarra. *Lati-*

fundismo y especulación: Notas para la historia agraria de Isla de Pinos (1900–1958). Serie Isla de Pinos 23. Havana: Instituto de Historia, Academia de Ciencias de Cuba, 1968.

Roig de Leuchsenring, Emilio. *Historia de la Enmienda Platt.* Havana: Editorial de Ciencias Sociales, 1973.

Scott, James Brown. *Cuba, la America Latina, los Estados Unidos.* Havana, 1926.

Sorhegui, Arturo. "Isla de Pinos: Apuntes." University of Havana, July–December 1978.

Stevenson, Robert Louis. *Treasure Island.* 1883. New York: Airmont Books Classic, 1962.

Stubbs, Jean. *Cuba: The Test of Time.* London: Latin America Bureau, 1989.

Suri Quesada, Emilio. "Cazafortunas Peggy." *Juventud Rebelde,* 26 November 1989.

Sutherland, Elizabeth. *The Youngest Revolution.* New York: Dial Press, 1969.

Szulc, Tad. *Fidel: A Critical Portrait.* New York: William Morrow, 1986.

Terry, T. Philip. *Terry's Guide to Cuba, Including the Isle of Pines.* Boston: Houghton Mifflin, 1926.

Thomas, Hugh. *Cuba. The Pursuit of Freedom.* Updated edition. New York: Da Capo Press, 1998.

———. *The Slave Trade.* New York: Simon and Schuster, 1997.

Torriente Brau, Pablo de la. *La Isla de los 500 asesinatos.* Havana: Nuevo Mundo Ediciones, 1962.

———. *Presidio Modelo.* Havana: Ediciones Politicas, Editorial de Ciencias Sociales, 1969.

Torriente y Peraza, Cosme de la. *Mi misión en Washington, 1922–1925: La soberanía de la Isla de Pinos.* Havana: University of Havana, 1952.

Unterecker, John. *Voyager: A Life of Hart Crane.* New York: Farrar, Straus, and Giroux, 1969.

Weyler y Nicolau, Valeriano. *Mi mando en Cuba (10-2-1896–31-10-1987), tomo segundo (20 marzo a 10 octubre 1896).* Madrid: Imprenta Felipe González Rojas, cinco tomos, 1910–11.

Wright, Irene A. *Cuba.* New York: Macmillan, 1910.

———. *Isle of Pines.* Havana, 1910.

Index

Note: *Italicized page numbers indicate photographs.*

abusadora store, 146
Academy of Sciences (Isle), 161
Ackom, Alfred, xix, 132–33
Aerovias Q (airline), 90
agriculture: Castro's plans for, 99–100,
    105; co-ops in, 91, 101, 126–27; in
    depression, 58; description of, 27–29,
    31; farms seized, 71, 72, 101; housing
    for workers in, 115, 134, 136–37;
    markets for crops, 24–25, 55, 65, 72–73,
    137, 172n. 12; production in (1990s),
    151–56; reservoir's impact on, 29, 54,
    55, 101; schools linked to, 114–17;
    student workers in, 103–10. *See also*
citrus industry; fruit industry; land;
    ranching
alienation, increased, 159
All the Best in Cuba (Clark), 79
Almacigos Land Company, 21
Almeida, Juan, Sr., 87
Amalia (queen of Spain), 3
American Cemetery, *xviii,* 26–27
American Central School, 82
American Club, 26
American Federation (organization), 23
American occupation: demonstrations
    against, 22–23; general effects of, x;
    Isle of Pines's status under, 17–18, 20

American Settlers' Association, 21
Amistad con los Pueblos (school), 160
amnesty, 84–85, 86, 88
ANAP (National Association of Small
    Farmers), 100, 109
Anderson (Ind.), church missionary board
    in, 159
Angolans: assistance for, 117; education
    for, 115–16, 129, 131–32; prospects for,
    133
Animal Husbandry–Veterinary
    Polytechnical Institute, 131
annexation, 18, 20, 37–40
Anti-Imperialist League of the Americas,
    38–39
Antilleans, school for, 81
Army of Working Youth (EJT), 136,
    174n. 19
Auténticos (party), 78, 82

Baca, Belén, 81
Baca, José, 81
Baca Baca, Virginia, xix, 80–81, 154–55
Baire (boat), 104
Baker, Sylvia: background of, xvi, 52; on
    courtship, 52–53; death of, 156;
    immigration of, 51; occupation of, 53;
    photograph of, *xvii*; on shortages, 153;
    support group of, xiii, 54; visit to, 147
Baltimore American (newspaper), 22–23
Bamboo (hotel), 164
Banco de Fomento Comercial, 90
Bank for Economic and Social
    Development (BANDES), 89
Batista, Sgt. Fulgencio: coup by, 68–69, 83;
    economic development and, 89; election
    of, 69; fall of, 97; prisoners confront,
    86–87; status of, 78; World War II
    and, 70
Bayamo barracks, 83
Bay of Pigs, 104–5
Bayo Soto, Enrique, 38
Beals, Carleton, 16
Bentham, Jeremy, 50–51

Bérriz, Lt. Col. D. José, 8–9, 10
Betancourt, Rosendo, 7
Bibijagua (beach), 90
Bibijagua (hotel), 161
birds, preserve for, 164–65
blacks: prejudice against, 112; religion of,
    158; settlement of, xix, 80–81. *See also*
    Baca Baca, Virginia
Bohemia (weekly), 88
botanical gardens, 36, 79
Brazo Fuerte docks, 5–6
brickworks, damaged, 78
The Bridge (Crane), 44–45
Brooke, Gen. John R., 17–18
Browning, Robert, 61
businesses: bakery, 7, 148; catering to
    foreigners, 146; confiscation of, 100–
    101; foreign ownership of, 19, 25;
    garage/repair, 91; hardware store, 59,
    91; in 1990s, 144–46; shoe shine, *145*

Caballos, Mount, 3–4
La Cabaña fortress, 9, 10, 18, 84
Cadena, Marcos Alexis, 114
Capote, Juan M., 87, 98
Carballo, Amelia, xix–xx, 142, 143
Carbonell, Carlos, 18
Caribbean area, map of, *14*
Casaco (boat), 62
Castells, Pedro A., 66, 67–68
Castro, Raúl, 152
Castro Ruz, Fidel: background of, 82–83;
    goals of, 99–100, 145; imprisonment
    of, 83–88; Moncada Garrison attacked
    by, 8, 83, 84; reading of, 85–86;
    socialism of, 104–7; at theatrical
    performance, 113. *See also* post-
    Revolution Cuba
Cavalry Garrison, 65, 78–79
Cayman Islands immigrants: area chosen
    by, 32–35, 54, 56; language of, 25;
    marginalization of, 105; timing of
    arrival of, 51. *See also* Hydes, Dick;
    Jackson, Bertha Maud Tatum

Cayo Largo, as tourist spot, 163–64
cemetery, *xviii*, 26–27
ceramics industry, xix, 140–43. *See also*
  Wheeler, Harriet
Ceramics Technological Institute, 142
Cespedes, Carlos Manuel de, 174n. 22
Chibás, Eduardo, 82, 173n. 13
Chile, citrus joint venture with, 136
Chinese immigrants, 4
Chueaux, M., 3–4
churches: choices in, 26, 31, 53;
  construction of first, 2; damaged by
  hurricane, *41, 42,* 77–78; guerrillas and,
  145; importance of, 158–59; marble
  baptismal font for, 4; marriage in, 33;
  recreation center in, 75–78; schools
  associated with, 81–82
Church of God (Nueva Gerona), 53, 159
Cisneros Betancourt, Salvador, 11
Cisneros de la Torre, Caridad, 6
citrus industry: cultivation in, 26; exports
  of, 25, 134–36; grapefruit's importance
  in, 37, 134; processing in, *135;* surplus
  in, 152; workers and housing in, 115,
  136–37
Clara Zetkin (school), 119
Clark, Sydney, 79–80
Cochinito restaurant (Nueva Gerona), 145
Cocodrilo (south coast): description of
  (1990s), 147–48; fishing on, 33, 54; gas
  energy for, 156; immigrants to, 32–35,
  54, 56; playground in, *155;* remoteness
  of, 95–96; tourism investments in,
  162–63
Las Codornices Motel (see map 2), xix,
  161
Colina, Isora, 157, 161
Colina, Juan: assistance from, 144;
  children of, 161; home of, 107; on
  hospital, 157–58; occupation of, 105–6;
  on prison experience, 66–67
Colombo Bay docks, 4, 5–6
Los Colonos: housing in, 154–55; name of,
  6; settlers of, 81

Colony Hotel (see map 2): description of,
  89, 96; luncheon at, 149–50; meetings
  at, 113; tourism and, 99, 163
Columbus, Christopher, 1
Communist Party (Cuban): after socialist
  bloc demise, 143–44; Central
  Committee (CCCP) of, 137, 173n. 1,
  173–74n. 2; founder of, 39; on religion,
  158
Communist Youth League, 105, 108
community: under communism, 106–7;
  joint pig pen for, 153
construction industry: in American
  occupation, 19; funds for, 23; materials
  for, 139, 154–55; post-Revolution, 103,
  106, 112, 115–16
consumer goods, demands for, 133
Contino, Rev. Samuel, 159
cooking. *See* foodstuffs
Coolidge, Calvin, 39
Copernico (school), 119
Coppelia ice cream parlor (Nueva Gerona),
  106
Cossio Cisneros, Evangelina: annexation
  and, 39; exile of, 65; as heroine, 10, 16;
  imprisonment of, 9, 11; rescued from
  prison, 12–13, 18; uprising organized
  by, x, xii, 7–8, 145; on youth, 109
Cossio y Serrano, José Agustín, 6–7, 9
Cotorro (Parrot) Springs (Santa Fé), *89*
Council of Ministers, 173–74n. 2
Council of State, 173n. 1
Crane, Hart, 44–47
crime: low rate of, 50; post-Revolution,
  110–12, 145, 159; in World War II, 73.
  See also Model Prison
The Crime of Cuba (Beals), 16
Cristobal Colón (ship), 22
crocodiles, Cuban, 37, 147, 165
cruise ship lines, 162–63
Cuba: ambassadors of, 39; Constitution of,
  20, 69; election fraud in, 23; map of, *14;*
  sovereignty over Isle of Pines, 16, 18,
  20, 21, 37–40; in World War II, 69–70.

Cuba—*continued*
    See also Havana; post-Revolution
        Cuba; U.S.-Cuban relations
Cubana Airlines, 133, 149
A Cuban Amazon (Dunbar), 13
Cuban Institute of Friendship with the
    Peoples, 147
Cuban Olympic Committee, 173–74n. 2
Cuban Revolution: goals of, 99–100; Isle
    secured in, 97–99. *See also* post-
    Revolution Cuba; Twenty-Sixth of July
    Movement
Cuban Telephone Company, 78
Cuba (pamphlet), 21–22
Cuba (Thomas), 16
Cuba with Pen and Pencil (Hazard), 5

D'Alerta Soto, Victor Hugo, 84
Dampier, William, 2
"Daughter of the Caribbean" (Díaz),
    168–70
Davis, Arthur V., 90
day care facilities, 115, 156
Decker, Karl, 12
La Demajagua. *See* Santa Barbara
depression: difficulties in, 49, 64–65;
    ethnicity and, 70; prison during, 65–69;
    unemployment in, 48, 61
Díaz Blanco, Roberto, 168–70
Díaz Cartaya, Agustín, 86–87
Dina, José, xix, 132, 133
Dingley Act, 24
Dionisio Vives, Capt.-Gen. Francisco, 3
disease, 4–5, 93, 171n. 1. *See also* health
    care
doctors: blacks as, 95; mortality rates and,
    157–58; on-call, 26; quality of, 32. *See
    also* health care
Dodge, Merrill, 114
Dominican Republic, planned invasion
    of, 83
Drake, Francis, 2
droughts, 40, 65

Duarte, Nicolás, 2–3
Dunbar, Virginia Lyndall, 13

Ebanks, Anne (Annie) Yates: background
    of, xvi; marriage and family life of,
    55, 56–57; photograph of, *xvii;* visit
    to, 147
Ebanks, Rulle: background of, xvi; on
    community, 54–55; death of, 156;
    occupation of, 58, 110; photograph of,
    xvii; visit to, 147
Echevarría, Avelardo, 138
economic development: American
    occupation and, 20; under Batista, 89–
    90; land speculation in, 20, 21;
    organization for, 4. *See also* post-
    Revolution Cuba
economy: after socialist bloc demise, 136,
    143–49, 151–56, 159–60, 165–67;
    currency and, 107, 121, 133, 146, 161;
    impact on settlers, 40. *See also*
    depression
education: emphasis on, 114–17; problems
    in, 119–21, 131–32; self-directed, 19.
    See also schools
*The Eighteenth Brumaire of Louis
    Bonaparte* (Marx), 86
EJT (Army of Working Youth), 136,
    174n. 19
Ellejalde Villalón, Oscar, xix
El Mesón restaurant, 146–47
El Protector (ship), 18
El Retardao (music group), 58
L'Empire Américain (Julien), 16
energy sources, 153–56
environmentalism, tourism and, 37, 147,
    162–65
Escuela Secondaria Basica en el Campo
    (ESBEC), 115, 133, 134, 136–37
"Eternity" (Crane), 45–47
ethnicity, 54, 69–70. *See also* blacks;
    race
Evangelina Cossio Primary School, 78, 79

Experimental Ceramics Workshop, 142–43, 161
exports: agricultural, 24–25, 134–36, 172n. 12; curtailment of, 40

Farmers and Growers Cooperative Telephone Exchange, 26
Fasser, Inez, 92, 102–3
La Favorita Hotel (Nueva Gerona), 38
La Fé. *See* Santa Fé
Ferdinand VII (king of Spain), 3
Fernández, Capt. Braulo, 62
Fernández Alvarez, José Ramón, 97–98, 173–74n. 2
Fernández Fala, Manuel, xix, 131–32, 133
Fernández García, Serafín, 9–10, 18–19, 30
Fernández Soto, Andrés: on American occupation, 18–19; background of, xii; on Cavalry Garrison building, 78–79; on Cossio's uprising, 9–10, 16; on free port status, 91, 100; home of, 30; photograph of, *xii*; on Sundstrom's bungalow, 154
Finlay, Carlos, 171n. 1
fires, 164–65
fishing industry, 33, 54, 120, 166
Florida Department of Agriculture, 25
flour, import of, 148, 153
foodstuffs: illness and, 93; imports of, 148, 153; *majá* boa as, 5; markets and, 146; post-Revolution, 121; shortages and, 152–54; for students, 132
Forrest, Augustus (Gus): courtship of, 52–53; occupation of, 51, 54, 55, 58, 109–10
Forrest, Sylvia Adina Baker. *See* Baker, Sylvia
Fortescue, G. R., 23–24
Four Corners school, 81
Franco, Dionisio, 3
fruit industry: pineapples, 24–25; reservoir's impact on, 55; seasonality

and, 44; wages in, 63; watermelons, 147, 152; workers for, 34. *See also* citrus industry

Gaines, William Jones, 110–12
gallego, use of term, 19
Gallego Club, 19
Garay, Sindo, 10
García, Daniel: as art teacher, 140, 141, 142; background of, xix–xx; market decorations and, 146
Gaviota tourism group, 162
gender, foreign students by, 129. *See also* women
Genpower Cuba S.A., 156
Geography Congress (1942), 70
German Democratic Republic (East Germany), ceramics industry and, 141–42
Germany: immigrants from, 70–71; U-boats of, 74
Ghanaians, education for, 132–33
gold, search for, 3–4
Gómez, Gen. Máximo, 8, 11
Gómez house (Nueva Gerona), 10, 41
González, Rosa, 58
González Vines, Rolando, 111–12, 145
Goodman, Benny, 96
Granma landing, 97
Granma (newspaper), 121
Grapefruit Festival, 134
Grau San Martín, Ramón, 69, 78–79, 82
Great Britain: island ownership and, 2; visits to, 93–94. *See also* Rice, Margaret (Peggy) Pitman
Guanahatabey Indians, 2, 162
Guanajay, prison in, 84
Guantánamo Naval Base, 42, 45, 48, 171n. 3
guerrilla movement, name of, 174n. 16
Guevara, Ernesto (Che), 106, 115, 139
Guiteras Holmes, Antonio, 69, 173n. 6
Gulf Caribbean Tourist Circuit, 89

Hanzawa, Eduardo, xix, 126–27
Harada, Kesano: background of, xiv; on
 Castro's impact, 102; death of, 156;
 marriage and family of, 64–65, 71, 73,
 125–26; photograph of, xvi; visit to, 147
Harada, Mosako: background of, xiv; on
 Castro's impact, 101; citizenship of, 74;
 family of, 125–26; on farming, 64–65,
 91, 152; on hurricane, 43; imprison-
 ment of, 70–73; photograph of, xvi; visit
 to, 147
Hart, Elizabeth Belden, 44
Hart Davalos, Armando, 97–98, 173n. 1
Havana: art school in, 140, 142; ceramics
 group in, xix, 142, 143; harbor in, 62; as
 market, 6, 55; shopping in, 92; Women's
 Prison in, 9, 11
Hawkins, John, 2
Hay, John, 21
Hay-Quesada Treaty: opposition to, 22–
 23, 38, 39; ratification of, 39–40;
 support for, 16, 38–39
Hazard, Samuel, 5, 36
health care: free, 118–19, 123–24;
 improvements in, 157–58; in prison, 72.
 See also doctors
Hearst, William Randolph, 7–8, 12, 16
Hemingway, Ernest, 74
Hernández, Bruno, 9–10
Hernández, Melba, 83
Hernández (Goyo), Gregorio, 90
Hibiscus Club, 26
Hill, James A., 25, 35
History Will Absolve Me (Castro), 83, 88
Honecker, Erich, 141
hospitals: childbirth in, 63; modernization
 of, 32, 144, 157–58; name of, 104; staff
 of, 95. See also doctors
housing: for agricultural workers, 115,
 134, 136–37; development of, 144;
 materials for, 154–55; scarcity of, 107;
 for student workers, 107–8. See also
 Sundstrom, Edith Larson, bungalow of
Hugo, Victor, 86

hurricanes: in 1907, 41; in 1915, 41; in
 1917, 41–42; in 1926, 40–41, 43, 44–47,
 48–49; in 1932, 173n. 3; in 1944, 77–78,
 91; in 1966 (Alma), 105; Crane's poem
 on, 45–47; impact on settlers, 40;
 prisoners during, 68
Hydes, Dick, xiv, xv, 35, 147
Hydes, William, 35

immigration: after revolution, 109; after
 World War I, 28; diversity in, 19;
 motivation for, 27. See also specific
 places of origin and specific individuals
independence, 11–13, 16. See also Cuban
 Revolution; War of Independence
industrialization, increased, 99, 139–43
infrastructure: Castro's plans for, 100;
 energy sources and, 153–56;
 improvements in, 25–26, 90–91, 103–7;
 telephone services and, 26, 78, 154–55.
 See also transportation
INRA (National Institute of Agrarian
 Reform), 88
International Red Cross, 72
International Telephone and Telegraph
 Company, 78
irrigation systems, 136, 137. See also
 reservoirs
Isla de la Juventud. See Isle of Youth
Isla de la Juventud (ferry), 148–49
La Isla de los 500 asesinatos (Torriente),
 66, 84, 173n. 6
Isla de Pinos (Nuñez Jiménez), 16
Island Development Society, 4
Islands in the Stream (Hemingway), 74
Isle of Pines: boosters of, 4–6, 21–22;
 climate of, 15; diversity of, 19, 32, 62; as
 dumping ground, 4, 80; early history of,
 1–7; as free port, 89–91, 99–100; legal
 status of, 16, 18, 20, 21, 24, 25, 37–40;
 northern part described, 27–32, 51. See
 also American occupation; Cocodrilo
 (south coast); Isle of Youth; pineros;
 post-Revolution Cuba

Isle of Pines Appeal (weekly): on annexation, 37–38, 40; founding of, 20; on Gallego Club, 19

Isle of Pines Bank, 25

Isle of Pines Company, 20

Isle of Pines drink, 37, 136

Isle of Pines Hotel (Nueva Gerona), 88

Isle of Pines Ice and Electric Company, 25–26

Isle of Pines Land Development Company, 21

Isle of Pines Steamship Company, 22, 25, 36, 90

Isle of Pines Transportation and Supply Company, 20

Isle of Youth: approach to, ix–xi; maps of, 14, 15; mortality on, 156–58; name of, ix, 106, 115, 119; northern vs. south coast, 147; poetry about, 168–70. *See also* Isle of Pines

Italian immigrants, hostility toward, 70–71

J. P. Morgan and Company, 39

Jackson, Atkin, xiv, 33, 35, 42, 147

Jackson, Bertha Maud Tatum: background of, xiv; on hurricane, 42–43; on immigration, 32–33; photograph of, *xv*; on transportation, 34; visit to, 147

Jackson, Elizabeth, 35

Jackson, Lydia, 42

Jackson, William Moddriel, xiv, 33, 34, 35, 42

Jacksonville, name of, 33, 35. *See also* Cocodrilo (south coast)

Jamaican immigrants, 25, 51. *See also* Baker, Sylvia

Japanese Association, 126, 127

Japanese immigrants: Castro's plans and, 100, 101–2; colony of, 19, 91, 101, 126–27; imprisonment of, 70–74; separateness of, 64; as workers, 43. *See also* Harada, Kesano; Harada, Mosako

Joliet (Ill.), prison in, 50, 114

Jones's Jungle (botanical gardens), 36, 79

Jordine brothers, 51, 54

Júcaro, hurricane in, 43

judicial system: humanitarian judge in, 80; murder trial and, 111–12, 145; parole and, 113–14

Julien, Claude, 16

kaolin processing plant, 139

Keenan, Thomas, 21

Kennedy, John F., 104–5

Khrushchev, Nikita, 104–5

Koenig, Gertrude, 27

Koenig, Harry: background of, xiii, 27–28; business of, confiscated, 100–101; death of, 156; on hurricane, 48–49; land of, 91; on markets, 146; photograph of, *xiii*; on shortages, 153–54

Koenig, Hermine, 27–28

Koenig, J. M., 27

Koenig, John (Harry's brother), 27

Koenig, John (Harry's father), 27–28

Koenig, Paul, xiii, 27, 48

Koenig, Stefania, 27, 28

Koenig, William (Willy), xiii, 27, 28, 154, 156

Kometa (hydrofoil), 103

Koritsky, Aaron, 38, 59

land: Castro's plans for, 100, 101; confiscation of, 71, 72, 101; for expanding farms, 91; handed down, 55, 81; speculation in, 20–21, 35. *See also* agriculture

language: disappearance of English, 123–25; disappearance of Japanese, 125–27; learning, 28, 82, 124; maintaining English, 127; prevalence of Cuban Spanish, 129

Lanier Swamp, 32, 147

Larson, Astrid Maria, 30

Larson, Oskar, 30

Laureal Slevin, E. de, 37–38, 40

Lee, Maj.-Gen. Fitzhugh, 11, 17–18

leisure activities: absence of, 128; dances, 52–53, 54, 56, 76–77; facilities for, 74–78, 90; food and games in, 62–63; for students, 108, 129, 132; swimming, 28; for tourists, 162–63. *See also* churches; music; social life

Lens y de Vera, Eduardo, 70

Leyva Zamora, Marcelino, 111–12, 145

La Libertad a tres pasos (play), 113

livestock, individuals' raising, 152–53. *See also* ranching

Lutheran Church School (Nueva Gerona), 124

Luz Hernández, José, 4–5

Maceo, Gen. Antonio: death of, 11; school and, 115; supporters of, 7, 8–10

Machado, Gerardo: election of, 40; fall of, 68, 173n. 6; Model Prison and, 51; prisoners of, 65, 69, 172n. 20

Magoon, Charles E., 23, 78

Maine (ship), 16

Main Square (Nueva Gerona), 145

"The Mango Tree" (Crane), 44

Manrique de Rojas, Hernán, 2

marble quarries, 3–4, 78

Marmolsol, description of, 136–37

Martí, José, 6, 11, 80, 86

Marx, Karl, 86

Mayal Arteaga, José Antonio, xix, 160–61

Mayal Valdés, Yaqueline (Jackie), *xviii*, xix, 165–67

McKinley, William, 11–13, 16, 172n. 17

McKinley Fruit Growers' Association, 25

McPherson, Lydia, xix, 123–25

Medina, Waldo, 80, 87–89

Mella, Julio Antonio, 39–40, 172n. 20

Miller, Capt. J. A., 24–25

Mills, Robert, 49

Mills, Capt. William J., 25, 36, 90

Mi Mando en Cuba (Weyler), 39

Minato, Ykio, 71

mineral springs: benefits of, 4–5, 158; facilities for, 36, *89*

Les Misérables (Hugo), 86

Model Prison: condemnation of, 80; construction of, 50–51; context of, x–xi; deactivation of, 99, 114; librarian and library for, 81, 84–85; as museum, 139; parole from, 113–14; photographers for, 84; photograph of, 52; political prisoners in, 65–66, 68, 84–88, 95, 104, 113; praise for, 79; prisoners abused in, 66–68; prisoners' protests at, 86–87; rebels' victory at, 97–99; theater group in, 113–14; wartime prisoners in, 70–73

Molina, Leonor, 13

Moncada Garrison, 8, 83, 84, 173n. 15

Monroe Doctrine, 17

Montané, Jésus (Chucho), 84, 95

Montané, Sergio, 84–85, 87

Morgan, Henry, 2

Morro Castle, 5–6, 62

mortality, 156–58

Mozambicans, education for, 115–16, 129, 132, 133

murders, 110–12, 145

music: in churches, 53; favorite songs and, 76; in prisoners' protest, 86; *rumba*, 57; in social life, 31; *sucu-suco*, 56–58, 172–73n. 2. *See also* leisure activities

My Life So Far (Rice), 60–61

Namibians, education for, 129

National Association of Small Farmers (ANAP), 100, 109

National Institute of Agrarian Reform (INRA), 88

National Men's Prison. *See* Model Prison

National Sports Commission, 90

New York Globe (newspaper), 22

New York Journal: on Cossio's rescue, 12–13; on Cossio's uprising, 7–8, 11; on independence, 16

Norniella Santos, Angel, xix–xx, 141–43

Nuestra Señora de los Dolores Church (Nueva Gerona), 4, 42, 145, 158

Nueva Gerona: airport in, 90; boats in, 120; Castro's speech in, 99–100, 145; churches in, 4, 31, 41, 42, 53, 145, 158–59; clubs in, 26; concert in, 144; construction of, 4; demonstrations in, 22–23, 38–39; description of (1990s), 144–46; founding of, 3; hospital in, 63, 95, 144, 157; hotels in, 38, 88; housing in, 29–30; hurricane damage in, 41–43, 78; mayor of, 60; Mother's Day cakes in, 148; restaurants in, 59, 145; schools in, 114, 124; tourism in, 36; uprising in, 8–9; women's prison in, 65
Nueva Gerona Amnesty Council, 84–85
Nuñez Jiménez, Antonio, 16

occupations: combining multiple, 19, 26–28; education and, 160–61; post-Revolution, 124–25; south coast vs. northern, 51; in World War I, 61; for youth, 63, 103–10, 114–17
O'Donnel, Capt.-Gen. Leopoldo, 4
Operation Vulture, 120–21
oral histories, overview of, xi–xx
organizations: for development, 4; literary and social, 26. See also churches; Twenty-Sixth of July Movement
Oropresa, Zenaida, 84–85
Ortodoxos (party), 82

Pablo de la Torriente Brau (school), 119
Palma Soriano (freighter), 148–49
La Paloma (boat), 34
Panama Canal, disease and, 171n. 1
Parliament, constitution adopted by, 69
Parrot (Cotorro) Springs (Santa Fé), 89
Pearcy, Edward J., 24, 53
Pearcy, Samuel H., 20–21, 35
Pearcy, Vera Wheeler, 53
Pearcy family, cemetery plot of, 27
Pearcy v. Stranahan, 24
Pearl Harbor, attack on, 69–70
penal colony, 6–7, 62. See also Model Prison; prisoners

Pepe el Mallorquín, 3
Pilar (yacht), 74
Pimienta family, 10
pineapple growing, 24–25
pineros: literacy of, 10, 81, 115; name of, 9; nostalgia of, 137; resilience of, 160; return home after war, 18. See also specific individuals
Pinero (ship), 48–49, 88
Pioneer Headquarters, 114
pirates, 2–3, 37
Platt, Orville H., 20
Platt Amendment, 20, 69, 173n. 6
Playa Girón (Bay of Pigs), 104–5
Poey, Felipe, 5
Pole Isla (company), 136–37
politics: ethics and, 82–83; prisoners and, 65–66, 68, 84–88, 95, 104, 113; social issues in, 78. See also annexation; Cuban Revolution; independence
Popular Power (municipal government), 153, 155
population: in 1792, 2–3; in 1835, 3; in 1868–78, 6; in 1901, 18; in 1907, 21; in 1919, 21, 65; in 1931, 65; in 1978, 119; in 1996, 156; in 2000, 15; changes in, 51; diversity of, 19; in 1960s, 109
Porro Gener, Pablo, 138
post-Revolution Cuba: agricultural work in, 103–10, 114–17; alienation and resilience in, 159–61; Bay of Pigs and, 104–5; citrus industry in, 134–37; crime and justice in, 110–12, 113–14, 145; dairy improvements in, 137–39; education in, 119–21; food production in, 151–56; foreign student program in, 115–16, 129–34; industrialization in, 139–43; language changes in, 123–28; mortality in, 156–58; quality of life in, 143–49, 165–67; study and work in, 114–19
Presidio Modelo. See Model Prison
Presidio Modelo (Torriente), 66

prisoners: characteristics of, 65–66; health care for, 72; occupations of, 4, 79; rights of, 69; training and education for, 71–72. *See also* Model Prison; penal colony

Pro–Isle of Pines Defense Column, 38

Pro–Isle of Pines Patriotic Committee, 38

prostitution, 68

Puerto Rico, U.S. control of, 17

Punta del Este, 33, 162

Punta Francés, 162–63

quality of life: in 1990, 143–49; in 1999, 165–67

Quesada, Gonzalo de, 21

race, 6, 94. *See also* blacks; ethnicity

Rachek, Ramón, xiii, 28, 29

Rachek, Vasily, xiii, 28–29

Radio Caribe, 106

ranching: Castro's plans for, 99–100; fencing for, 152; illegal slaughter in, 137, 152; improvements in dairy, 137–39; slavery and, 6

Rancho del Tesoro Hotel (see map 2), 161

Raynard, Charles, 23, 24

Rebel Army, 97, 104. *See also* Cuban Revolution

recreation center (WWII), 74–78

Reed, Walter, 171n. 1

reeducation, in prison, 113–14

reforestation, 97, 164

Reina Amalia (colony), settling of, 3, 6, 80–81

Relatives' Amnesty Committee for Political Prisoners, 88

Remington, Frederic, 13

remittances, from abroad, 166–67

reservoirs: impact on agriculture of, 29, 54, 55, 101; inauguration of first, 106–7

Revolutionary Armed Forces (FAR), 174n. 19

Reyes, Magaly: assistance of, 144, 157;

children of, 107, 161; on energy, 155, 156; as student worker, 105–7

Rice, Derek, 61, 92

Rice, Harry: birth of, 61; departure of, 103; illness of, 92, 96; school buddy of, 84, 95; sister of, 94, 118

Rice, Joan: background of, xix; birth of, 63; death of, 117–18; living situation of, 111; marriage and divorce of, 94, 96, 116; during World War II, 74, 77; youth of, 92–93, 94, 95

Rice, Margaret (Peggy) Pitman: background of, xix; on Castro, 103; on crime, 111; death of, 151, 156, 165; friends of, 60, 122–23; ill health of, 118–19; marriage and family life of, 60, 62–63, 92, 96, 111, 118; memoirs of, 60–61; ninetieth birthday of, 149–51; occupations of, 74–78, 92–93, 102–3; photographs of, *xviii*; travel of, 93–94; on treasure hunting, 61–62, 63–64, 79; visit to, 147

Rice, Maurice: marriage and separation of, 60, 63–64, 92; treasure hunting and, 61–62, 79

Rivas, José, 3

Rives, Mongo: background of, xvi, 172–73n. 2; cruise ships and, 163; photograph of, *xvii*; on *sucu-suco*, 57–58

Roa, Raúl: island's renaming and, 119; library supported by, 85; on prison experience, 67–68; radical politics of, 65–66

Rojas y Avellaneda, Jerónimo, 2

Roosevelt, Theodore, 11, 37, 172n. 17

Root, Elihu, 20, 23, 24

Rosa, Alexis, 122–23, 151

Royal Air Force, 74

Ruíz, Luis, 138

St. Joseph's Academy (later San José Academy, Nueva Gerona), 82

San Alejandro Art School (Havana), 140, 142
Sánchez, Juan Manuel, 22–23
Sanitation Department, 38
San José Company, 21
Santa Ana, feast of, 8
Santa Barbara: farms in, 27–28, 51, 91; school in, 81; tourism in, 36
Santa Cruz del Sur, hurricane in, 68, 173n. 3
Santa Fé: clubs in, 26; founding of, 3; hotel in, 36, 90; hurricane in, 77–78; mineral springs in, 4–5, 89, 158; recreation center in, 74–78; schools in, 114, 160; tourism in, 36; uprising and, 8–10
Santa Fé Hotel, 90
Santa Fé Land Company, 21
Santamaría, Abel, 84
Santamaría, Haydée, 83, 84
Santa Rita Springs Hotel (Santa Fé), 36, 90
Santería, 158
Sardá, Maj. José María, 5–6, 21
Sardiñas, Father Guillermo, 145
schools: American, 28, 32, 81, 82; art courses in, 140, 141; for blacks, 81; boarding, 114–17, 160; community activities in, 54; English classes in, 127–28; for foreign students, 115–16, 129–34; hurricane damage to, 78; in prison, 68, 71–72; problems in, 119–21, 131–32; secondary, 81, 115–16, 119–20; tuition for, 63
Seneca (ship), 12
Shangri-La guest house (Patria), 92–93, 102
Siguanea Bay: docks in, 23–24, 135–36; turtle fishing in, 33
Simpson, Sarah, 44, 45
slavery, 6, 174n. 22
Slevin (American), 38
smuggling, 90, 91
soap operas, addiction to, 155, 166, 167
Social Defense Code (1938), 69

socialist bloc, demise of: economic problems of, 136, 159–60; food production difficulties and, 153; quality of life after, 143–49, 165–67
social life: components of, 26–27; destructuring of, 160–61. See also leisure activities
social services, 99, 160. See also health care
Sonny Boy (musician), 57–58, 172–73n. 2
Soviet Union (USSR), Cuba's link to, 104–5. See also socialist bloc, demise of
Spain: Civil War in, 66; heritage of, 19; island control and, 1–2, 17; U.S. opposition to, 11–12, 16
Spanish-American War (1898), 17. See also American occupation
Squiers, George, 22
SS Reina del Mar (ship), 93
Stateville Prison (Joliet, Ill.), 50, 114
Stevenson, Robert Louis, 3, 37, 172n. 16
students: criticism of, 108–9; demands for consumer goods, 133; influence of, 119; language used by, 129; name change proposed by, 106; number of, 130, 134; overview of, xix; prison visited by, 87, 104; program for foreign, 115–16, 129–34; study and work combined for, 114–17; as workers on Isle, 103–10
Students' Directorate, 68–69
sucu-suco, character and development of, 56–58, 172–73n. 2
sugar industry, 49, 172n. 21
Sundstrom, Albert: citizenship of, 60; courtship of, 31; death of, 121–22; occupations of, 58–59, 91–92, 102
Sundstrom, Edith Larson: on annexation, 40; background of, xiii–xiv; bungalow of, xiv, 29–30, 53, 154; on businesses, 91; departure of, 30, 122–23; friends of, 62; gift from, 150–51; on immigration, 30–31; on occupations, 58–59; on post-Revolution changes, 102, 121–22; on shopping, 92; on social life, 31–32
Sundstrom, Gunner, 60

Tatum, Edwina, 32–33
Tatum, Temper, 32–33
taxes: elimination of, 89–91; referendum on, 99–100; request for back, 101; on sea sand, 4
Teachers' Training College, 119, 129
telephone services, 26, 78, 154–55
Teller Amendment, 16
Ten Years' War, 5
Terracota 4 (ceramics group), xix, 142, 143
Terry's Guide (1926), 36
Texas Oil Company, 91
theater, prison group for, 113–14
Thomas, Hugh, 16
tile works: hurricane damage to, 78; production in, 5–6; workers for, 113–14
timber industry, 34, 35
tobacco industry, 24, 137
Torriente Brau, Pablo de la, 66, 84, 119, 173n. 6
Torriente y Peraza, Cosme de la, 16, 39
tourism: animals as draw in, 37, 138–39; under Batista, 92; under Castro, 99, 105, 161–65; fishing and, 96; hotels for, 161–62; investments in, 89–90; landmarks for, 79–80; limitations on, 174n. 26; mineral springs and, 4–5, 36, 89, 158; piracy legends and, 37
transportation: airplane, 80, 90, 133, 149; automobile, 26; bicycle, 150; boat, 34, 48–49, 62–63; Cuba to Isle of Pines, 18, 36, 48, 103, 148–49; of grapefruit, 135–36; horseback, 26, 31; military, 74–75; plans for, 23–24; roads for, 32, 95–96; tobacco industry and, 24; U.S. to Isle of Pines, 20
treasure hunting, allure of, 61–64, 79
Treasure Island (Stevenson), 3, 37, 172n. 16
Treaty of Paris, 17, 20
Trujillo, Rafael, 83
Tumbita Criolla (group), xvi, xvii, 163, 172–73n. 2. See also sucu-suco

Tupac Amaru Junior High School, 117, 119, 128
"Twenty-Sixth of July" (Díaz), 86
Twenty-Sixth of July Movement: founding of, 88; organization of, 98–99; underground branches of, 95; victory of, 97. See also Cuban Revolution

Ubre Blanca (White Udder), 138–39
Ukrainian immigrants. See Rachek, Vasily
unemployment, 48, 61, 160–61
United Railroads of Havana, 18, 21–22
United States: Cuba attacked by, 104–5; hegemony of, 17; as market for fruits, 24–25, 40; settlers from, 20, 21–22, 25, 29, 32, 40; settlers' return to, 48; visitors from, 36–37, 104. See also Koenig, Harry; Sundstrom, Edith Larson
U.S.-Cuban relations: Bay of Pigs and, 104–5; Isle's status and, 16, 20, 21, 37–40; World War II and, 69–70
U.S. Declaration of War on Spain, 16
U.S. Senate, influences on, 22–23, 39
United Victory Workers' Club, 74
University of Havana, 82–83, 125, 126
Upton's Restaurant (Nueva Gerona), 59
USS Milwaukee (ship), 45
USSR (Soviet Union), Cuba's link to, 104–5. See also socialist bloc, demise of

Valdés, Pepe, 95–96
Valdés Rice, Margarita (Shug): background of, xix; birth of, 96; on concert, 144; fuel shortage and, 153; gifts for, 150; home of, 165–67; on mother's death, 117–18; photograph of, xviii; on schooling, 116–17, 127–28
Valdés Rivas, Armando de Jesús: activism of, 95, 117; background of, xix, 95;

marriage and divorce of, 94, 96, 116;
photograph of, *xviii*
Los Van Van (Go-Go, music group), 144,
145
Vargas, Emilio, 7, 10
Victoria (weekly), 106, 144
Viet Nam Heroico (reservoir), 106–7
Villa Gaviota (see map 2), 162
Vinageras, Rosa, 3

wages, 63, 107, 112
War of Independence: annexation and, 39;
declaration of first, 174n. 22;
deportation to Isle during, 6–7; impact
on development, 4; U.S. newspaper on,
7–8, 11–13. *See also* Cossio Cisneros,
Evangelina
weaving, 56
Weyler, Lt.-Gen. Valeriano, 5, 8, 11, 12, 39
Weyler's Spring, 5
Wheeler, Harriet Powell: annexation and,
38–40; ceramics of, 38, 40, 51, 53, 54,
139; hurricane and, 40–41
wild life, preservation of, 37, 147, 162–65
Wilkins, Aldah, 93

Willis, A. E., 20
women: exile of, 65; health care for, 118;
imprisonment of, 9, 11, 83, 84;
occupations of, 61, 137
Women's Federation, 113
Wood, Gen. Leonard, 20, 37, 172n. 17
workforce: consciousness of, 109; students
as, 103–10, 114–17. *See also*
occupations
World Festival of Youth and Students
(1997), 131
World War I, 28, 40, 61
World War II: ethnicity and, 69–70;
imprisonment of Japanese in, 70–74;
recreation center during, 74–78
World Youth Festival (1978), 119
Wright, Irene, 22

Yamanashi (farmer), 64
yellow fever, 171n. 1

Zayas, Alfredo, 39–40
Zeidler, Ilse Sperlin, 110–12
Zetkin, Clara, 119
Zimbabweans, education for, 129

Jane McManus is an American writer, editor, and translator who has researched and written about Cuba during thirty years as a resident of Havana. Her articles have appeared in general, cultural, and travel publications in the United States, Europe, and Cuba. She is the author of the travel guide *Getting to Know Cuba* (1989).